SURVEILLANCE, SECURITY
AND SOVEREIGNTY

How a Peace Campaign Challenged the
Activities of a US Base in Britain

Chris – I thought this
might remind you of
your CND days!
Love webb

SURVEILLANCE, SECRECY AND SOVEREIGNTY

£3.50

How a Peace Campaign Challenged the
Activities of a US Base in Britain

Margaret L Nunnerley

© Margaret L Nunnerley, 2014

Published by Burley Publications

A CIP catalogue record for this book is available from the British Library.

ISBN 978-0-9928406-0-0

Book layout and cover design by Clare Brayshaw

Cover image © Matt Cryto Wikimedia Commons

Prepared and printed by:

York Publishing Services Ltd
64 Hallfield Road
Layerthorpe
York YO31 7ZQ

Tel: 01904 431213

Website: www.yps-publishing.co.uk

Contents

FOREWORD BY
PROFESSOR PAUL ROGERS

For twenty years a small group of dedicated and committed peace campaigners has endeavoured to throw light on the activities of United States intelligence and security agencies in the United Kingdom. Much of the focus has been on the Menwith Hill base near Harrogate in North Yorkshire, not least on the surprising way in which it has actually grown in size since the end of the Cold War – the opposite of what might have been expected.

The Campaign for the Accountability of American Bases (CAAB) has had three distinctive features. The first is the issue of "accountability" – the persistent demand to know what is being done on UK soil in what is actually listed as an RAF station but dominated by US personnel. For more than thirty years there have been indications that Menwith Hill connects into many elements of communications within the UK, and that it has a capability for gathering economic and business intelligence, but one of the most notable features of the whole experience has been the wall of silence which has so often blocked reasonable enquiries. CAAB has worked hard over the years to break this wall, often working with sympathetic MPs and academics. In doing so it has thrown much light on Menwith Hill and other US facilities, including their potential role in the controversial issue of missile defence.

The second is the nonviolent nature of the campaign. Those involved, especially Lindis Percy and Annie Rainbow, have studiously avoided any kind of violent confrontation. It is a stance stemming very much from their own beliefs but has also served to make it more difficult for those in authority to dismiss their many reasonable requests.

The third relates to the many problems of harassment and arrests experienced by CAAB, with this leading on to protracted court cases. These have resulted in the accumulation of a veritable wealth of experience, much of it concerning the conduct and accountability of US and Ministry of Defence personnel, but also relating to the military control of land. The legal fights have been personally costly but have a significance that goes well beyond Menwith Hill and other bases. Indeed they frequently relate directly to the state of civil liberties in the UK.

This carefully researched and thoughtful book has many qualities. It is a substantial contribution to the understanding of nonviolent direct action and its values, very much within the Quaker tradition, and it also throws plenty of light on US intelligence activities in Britain and how they relate to UK government policy. Finally, it is signally important in the context of civil liberties and how they may be eroded but, not least through groups such as CAAB, may be sustained and possibly enhanced. It will be of interest to a number of disparate groups: peace campaigners who want to reflect on a non-violent protest, its costs and effectiveness; lawyers who are concerned about our legal rights to peaceful protest, and MPs whose right to information is frustrated by a singularly secret government.

Since CAAB was established twenty years ago, and in parallel with its development, we have seen huge improvements in the social media but also a remarkably increased capacity for those in authority to monitor the activities of civil society, not least peace campaigners. At any time this book would have been a very valuable contribution but that last aspect makes it especially salient. It is an important read.

Paul Rogers
November 2012

INTRODUCTION

In 2008, a small group met at the Department of Peace Studies at Bradford University to discuss the current structure and working of the Campaign for the Accountability of American Bases (CAAB) given that, of the two key workers, one was unable to continue to work for the campaign because of ill health. The group, consisting of the remaining key worker, the Professor of Peace Studies and three members of the Society of Friends (Quakers) looked at structures, current challenges and long- term aims. One of the recommendations from the group was that action should be taken to ensure that the experience, achievements and knowledge which this campaign had amassed since beginning in the early 1990s should not be lost.

This research aims to record and analyse the spectrum of CAAB's activities during its first twenty years of campaigning (1992 to 2012), from its non-violent protests to its extensive and significant court campaigns. Although not primarily an academic study, the campaign is located in the following academic contexts: the study of conflict and its roots in society, the history and philosophy of non-violent action, the history of the development of liberty in Britain, and the legal framework in which the campaign operated. These are explored with the aim of giving the reader sufficient background to understand the broader issues without which some of the campaign's activities would be hard to evaluate. Consideration is also given to the history of the distinctive work for peace in the history of the Society of Friends (Quakers) since this is the expressed principle which informed the work of the campaigners. The main sources for this book are: the files of data recording the day-to-day activities of the campaign and particularly the court cases, correspondence with parliamentarians, with state agencies, and with organisations world-wide which have similar aims and concerns. Use is also made of the website material which includes periodic reports on significant events and copies of the regular newsletter.

It has been written with a mixed audience in mind. It will be of interest to groups or individuals who have developed principled non-violent methods of resistance to state policies to which they are strongly opposed, and who can find in this account information about the methods, principles, successes and failures of one particular campaign. At a time of significant shifts in world power there is renewed interest at a wider public level about Britain's place in the world at the start of the twenty-first century, particularly in the area of US/UK relations. For these readers, the information about the status and function of US bases in Britain will focus on aspects of the 'special relationship' which may prompt a reappraisal of its advantages and disadvantages for Britain, especially in light of Edward Snowden's revelations in 2013 about the extent of British/US surveillance activities and the inadequacies of democratic oversight and accountability.

The account concludes with a series of interviews with mainly sympathetic but objective outsiders to the campaign who offer detached views of its achievements.

Finally, questions which have arisen during the writing

of this account, and from interviews with outsiders and with the two campaigners, will be used as a basis for considering the future of the campaign.

Chapter 1

The Campaign: background and origins

It is important to acknowledge that the Campaign for the Accountability of American Bases did not originate solely from the concerns and convictions of one or two individuals. Before the two principal campaigners arrived in Yorkshire (Anni Rainbow in 1986 and Lindis Percy in 1990) there already existed organised local opposition to the presence and status of Menwith Hill. We know that concern and opposition to the presence and function of the base was expressed as early as the 1950s, and that more organised and vocal resistance emerged in the 1980s, partly inspired by the experience of the peace camps at Greenham Common but more importantly out of concern at the tension between East and West and the possibility of Cruise Missiles being sited at Greenham Common.

The group which emerged most clearly was the Otley Peace Action Group (OPAG). This group began in 1980, after a meeting called by Margaret and Michael McGowan, (later an MEP) which set out to discuss ways of co-ordinating local peace and disarmament initiatives in the Otley / Wharfedale areas. Within the first year they had over 100 members, the focus of their group being primarily to oppose the build-up of nuclear weapons, and to educate and organise local opinion against the proliferation of these weapons, while acting as a local information centre for all local organisations of like mind. The records show that in many ways they anticipated many of the methods of protest later adopted by CAAB. Notably, they produced a regular newsletter, held candlelit vigils, showed films such as John Pilger's 'The Peace Game', organised demonstrations (on one occasion police estimates placed the number attending a march to Menwith HIll at over 4000 people), held July 4th demonstrations and wrote to local MPs, the press and other local bodies. Although at first the main focus was not on Menwith Hill, from 1982 activities began to centre on the base and in 1983 OPAG set up the first of a series of weekend peace camps there; this was supported by numerous other local groups.

In 1984 a permanent Peace Camp was established on the A59 outside the base. This was a mixed camp (ie. not women only) and was supported by many local groups including OPAG. The activities of the peace campaigners on the camp again drew on the experience of Greenham, with acts of trespass and non-violence designed to test the laws which operated at the base, particularly the military land bye-laws. Two participants in the campaigning era of the 1980s and early 1990s, Anne Lee and Helen John have continued to campaign separately from CAAB, working closely with Yorkshire CND, but the records are insufficient to explore these activities in greater detail. Helen John, while in prison for protest activities at Menwith Hill, conceived the idea of starting a women-only peace camp, to replace the mixed camp.

The records show that by 1992 the group which in future would be known as CAAB had established itself as a separate campaign, a development which appears to be related to significant differences of principle and of campaigning activities. The CAAB campaigners recall this as being a very painful period, a time of repeated attempts to reach accommodation over ways of working. These years are not documented in the CAAB archives so it is possible only to allude to this time. By the early 1990s OPAG had closed, as had many other similar groups nationwide, following the fall of the Berlin Wall and the impact this had on the perceived threat from the Soviet Union.

CAAB's statement of aims and methods are set out on its website as: opposition to nuclear weapons, opposition to violent methods of resolving conflict, opposition to collusion with the US in its use of UK bases for the furtherance of nuclear activities. Its methods are: to use non-violent means of protest both at Menwith Hill and other US bases in Britain, with the aim of making transparent the use to which the bases are put, how they are run and to whom they are accountable; challenging the response to non-violent, legal protest at the bases, if necessary through the courts; sharing information with other peace campaigners, academics, politicians and any other individuals and public and advisory bodies who have an interest in the key issues. In this book the focus is on the activities at Menwith Hill, situated in North Yorkshire, the area in which both campaigners live, but there is documentation in the records of important non violent action and significant court campaigns that focus on other US bases in Britain.

Both the lead campaigners in CAAB, Lindis Percy and Anni Rainbow, have backgrounds of non- violent campaigning in Britain in the 1980s. Both were active in the Women's Peace campaign at Greenham Common, and Anni Rainbow in the protests against the war in Vietnam. Christine Dean, the current CAAB treasurer, was, as already noted, pivotal in setting up the Otley Peace Action Group (OPAG) in the early 1980's. Anni Rainbow is a Quaker. She was a Member first of Crawley Meeting in Sussex, then of Adel Meeting in Leeds, of Otley Meeting and now of Harrogate Meeting. Lindis Percy is not in membership but is an Attender at Harrogate Meeting, formerly at Southampton and Hull Meetings. In a statement in 'The Friend' (the Quaker weekly publication) Anni sets out her guiding principles and values:

'I am a Quaker and a peace campaigner. For me the two are indivisible. My faith embraces our historic Peace Testimony[1] and a tradition of non-violence and direct action. It is a faith that challenges me to work...for a fair, just, peaceful, open and caring society. It reminds me that as an individual I have a responsibility for the conduct of local, national and international affairs'.

The Quaker roots of CAAB and the nature of the contribution made by the Society of Friends are discussed in the next chapter.

CAAB, as detailed later, thus had a wider focus than opposing violence as a solution to problems or opposing the use of nuclear weapons. As the non-violent campaign progressed, and the arrests and court cases multiplied, the focus widened to embrace fundamental civil liberties issues about the right to peaceful protest, the legality of the laws invoked to stifle protest, the conduct of the Ministry of Defence police, the limits of peace campaigners' access to justice, and even broader issues of the reality of the power of parliament to scrutinise and oppose decisions made by the executive and to gain access to vital information when security and defence issues are involved. They discovered through experience the connections explored in academic peace literature[2] between the roots of violence and the political, social and legal structures of society, and in particular the importance of laying bare the ways in which these structures can sustain undemocratic and violent responses to social unrest and protest. CAAB is not unique in this, and a later chapter explores the links made with other non-violent protest movements which address the same issues.

It may be useful in view of the breadth and seriousness of these concerns to describe the organisational structure of CAAB which underpinned and sustained the activities of the peace campaigners. Essentially it is a modestly funded organisation with no paid staff, sustained by the voluntary activities of two peace campaigners who have for years been both activists, disseminators of information, networkers with other campaigners, civil rights activists requiring academic and political sophistication. This work was carried out in conjunction with family commitments and, in the case of one campaigner, a part-time professional job. Its base has been the home of one of the campaigners; its treasurer works on a voluntary basis, administering the regular donations from its network of supporters (about £1800 to £2000p.a). This can be supplemented by the occasional appeal, for example for legal funding for cases in which the campaigners have been involved. There is volunteer help for such important areas as the editing and printing of the CAAB newsletter, the setting up of the website that was initially financed by a charity and is now run by a volunteer, the monitoring of Planning Applications for Menwith Hill and Fylingdales, and, vital in the early years, powerful help and legal advice provided by a group of individual lawyers who shared the values and aims of the campaign. The importance of Legal Aid in funding lawful protest becomes clear in the description of the court campaign. With the recent cuts in Legal Aid Lindis Percy has had to appeal for money to support the costs and fines which accompanied the court cases in which she has been involved.

The most striking feature of CAAB is the absence of a formal organisational structure which can provide support, advice and challenge to the work of the campaign. There was initial discussion of the advantages and disadvantages of a formal structure with officers and membership, and this was rejected in favour of the looser structure which still exists. At the meeting described at the start of this paper, convened to consider the issues raised by the withdrawal from CAAB of one campaigner on health grounds, the subsequent vulnerability of the campaign was discussed, and suggestions made about how it might secure its achievements and plan for its development in a changing economic and political climate. In a later chapter comparisons will be made with Faslane 365, a campaign with comparable aims, values and methods, which will raise issues for campaigners about the type of organisational structure which is most useful to campaigns of this nature. At the time of writing, CAAB has one main campaigner, Lindis Percy, with a fellow Joint-Coordinator, together with a volunteer treasurer, a web master and a volunteer researcher who monitors Hansard.

It will be argued in this book that the activities of CAAB are rooted in the broad traditions of non-violent protest, and of testing and defining the reality of civil liberty in Britain. It is important at this stage, therefore to place the campaign in its historical and cultural context. There follows a brief discussion of the principles and practice which underlie both non-violent action and the struggle for civil liberties in Britain, and also the significance of the Quaker peace heritage that will help the reader to understand and evaluate the importance of the campaign activities described in the succeeding chapters. The focus is the status and function of US bases in Britain, although the records show that CAAB also has contacts with groups and individuals world-wide who are concerned with the presence of US Visiting Forces in their own countries.

Chapter 2

The Campaign in context

This chapter places the campaign in its historical and political context and is devoted to the discussion of two strands in the historic struggles for just and peaceful societies, that is, the engagement in non-violent action as a means of bringing about social change, and the struggle for political liberty. Both campaigners have also clearly located their campaigning in the context of their Quaker beliefs, and this connection is therefore explored in some detail in this chapter.

Non-violence. A dangerous idea?

Protesting but adhering to non-violent methods is an avowedly core value of CAAB, and it is useful to begin with a definition of this term, and to describe how key advocates and practitioners of this approach, such as Gandhi, Luther King and the Dalai Lama, have engaged in its key dilemmas. The Dalai Lama defines non-violence thus:

'Non-violence does not mean the absence of violence. It is something more positive, more meaningful than that. The true expression of non-violence is compassion, which is not just a passive emotional response, but a rational stimulus to action...(the) practice of non-violence depends entirely on the power of truth'[3].

He calls it an 'ancient and powerful idea' made familiar throughout the contemporary world by Mahatma Gandhi and Martin Luther King, applying the concept not only to politics but also to everyday life. The revival of the idea of non-violence in the twentieth century can be accounted for partly by the traumatic impact in Europe and the wider world of two world wars with their massive personal and economic cost. Something of the same response had occurred in the early years of the nineteenth century, after the prolonged and destructive years of the Napoleonic wars, when membership of newly founded Peace Societies grew, especially in Britain. But everyday experience and awareness of the world situation at the start of the twenty-first century raise important and searching questions about the concept and practice of non-violence, and the dilemmas that it raises. These questions are unavoidable as an analysis of CAAB develops.

Is non-violence more than a way of responding in a distinctive manner in a given conflict situation? Does it necessarily imply a revolution in social values, and, as Gandhi believed, a comparable inner revolution of a spiritual or religious nature? Does the concept of non-violence address only situations of conflict or does it also seek to address the structural foundations which lead to conflict, such as inequality, injustice, political oppression and the historical legacies of past cruelties and oppression? How does a belief in non-violence translate into action in a particular conflict situation? Importantly, we have to address issues of evaluation. Can we begin to say when and under what conditions it is an effective method of protest? What are the costs of this approach to the practitioners in situations where violence, destruction and cruelty are deliberate and calculated methods of achieving and maintaining power, or of settling historic disputes and grievances? Why is non-violent action seen as so dangerous to the established order, usually receiving contemptuous or violent responses?

These issues have been and continue to be debated and researched and reference is made to key sources in this debate[4]. The aim of this chapter is to clarify the debate sufficiently for the reader to understand the methods adopted by CAAB, to begin to reflect on the issues raised by the campaign, and to anticipate some of the difficulties of evaluation discussed at the end of this work.

When an attempt is made to define non-violence it is evident at once that the term simply defines itself only in opposition to the idea of violence. This at once conveys the idea of marginality, of rejection of a key human or societal quality but not a serious force in itself. Violence is the 'taken for granted' quality and non-violence simply a response to that quality. A helpful starting point is therefore to explore how peace theorists define and account for violence and our seemingly easy acceptance of its inevitability. Most writers on peace and non-violence attempt to define the sources of violence in society. Adam Curle, a peace academic who also worked in conflict situations in Nigeria, the Indian subcontinent and the Balkans, described what he called 'the three poisons'[5] which lie at the root of violence: wanting (or greed), jealousy, and hatred, all of which he argued, exercise powerful and ultimately destructive effects on the human mind. In another work[6], he moved onto a wider examination of the interconnectedness of the destructive forces of economic, political and military power. Curle argued that these are fuelled at all levels by the hope for power and profit, which produce a 'culture of violence'. He called this global phenomenon 'The Hydra' whose impact is violent or generating of violence, and went on to analyse the systems through which it operates. Curle's practical approach to this 'Hydra' was that we have to tame it, while also recognising the extent to which we are all part of it, and the difficulties of understanding its complexities. He argued that until we address this huge issue, our traditional methods of conflict resolution and of development planning are of limited use.

Curle was here describing, using metaphor and Buddhist philosophical terms, what other peace academics, in perhaps more accessible language, describe as the necessity to address the structural as well as the personal roots of violence. Lederach[7] argued for a 'transformative agenda which is concerned with broader social structures, moving towards a space for co-operation... and for non-violent mechanisms of handling conflict'. Fetherston[8] wrote that it is 'not enough to do something that assuages feelings of guilt and horror', but 'we have also to undertake an analysis of violent conflict which acknowledges how discourses and institutions in society serve to make violence and

11

violent conflict imaginable and understandable courses of action'. All these writers are therefore defining violence as not necessarily inherent in human nature, but as the by-product of economic, political and social systems that require challenge and control, but which are also sustained by our own internalisation of these values, which legitimises these systems. Curle argued that personal consciousness is therefore a vital component of change, that change comes when we alter reactions to violence, and that we have to step outside the systems of thought that generate and perpetuate the system, and develop different ways of thinking and communicating. In this he echoed Gandhi's reflections at the end of his life that he had failed to bring about the inner revolution in the members of the non-violent movement that he had inspired. It would be possible to see the history of post- independence India as vindicating Gandhi's assessment.

This analysis of how violence is generated enables us to have a realistic understanding of the forces which face non violent activists. It takes us some way to understanding one of the key discourses that sustains the activities and justifications of defence and military thinking, and in particular that justifies the presence and expansion at Menwith Hill. To an outsider, it seems perplexing, if not immoral that the US, and, in complicity, the UK, are prepared at a time of economic recession to spend billions on developing a world-wide and space based military deterrent against a threat which it is difficult to define. It is important to understand the fear and the determination to sustain dominance, leading to a policy of secrecy and violence that paradoxically contradict the values which they are aiming to protect. It explains, in part, why challenges and alternative ways of thinking are seen as dangerous, and explains also the personal costs of adopting a course of non-violent action. Gandhi believed that only the strongest and most disciplined person can practise it, and that opposing violent situations, structures, ideas and individuals requires a person to be 'strong and extraordinary'.

The history of non-violent action in modern Britain also demonstrates that Gandhi's realistic views are as relevant here as in twentieth century India. The personal cost to campaigners has been enormous, and as a former resister in World War Two made clear, 'anyone who says he is not afraid is either a liar or without imagination'[9]. As the description of the campaign will show, non-violent action brings the campaigner face to face with the realities of state power and of its abuses. This involves the campaigner in serious questions both of principle and of practice. What strategy best challenges structures and individuals that embody principles of repression and often illegality and democratic unaccountability? Is it ever possible or morally acceptable to try to live apart from the state system and to refuse to participate in it? How can campaigns working in non-violent ways avoid the splits and antagonisms that have characterised many twentieth century peace movements? What sort of organisation best supports campaigners in what we are beginning to see is an activity that is enormously demanding and that carries with it dilemmas that can, unchecked, lead to a perversion of its basic values?

What can an individual do that may have the power to influence a conflict or a potentially violent situation to achieve a different outcome? The spectrum of activities is wide and been adopted historically to meet a wide range of situations from challenging the inequality of black citizens of the US, to challenging the colonial rule of the British in India, to protesting against the building of motorways that threaten wildlife habitats. In the context of challenging the preparation and use of arms, and particularly of nuclear weapons, they have included a wide range of activities. Some have the straightforward aim of demonstrating opposition, for example holding silent vigils near military bases combined with articulating a reasoned and principled alternative that tries to engage public opinion and stimulate debate. Some will engage in direct action which aims to disrupt the activity which is the focus of the protest (for example lying down in a public highway to stop the transport of missiles or warheads). Another approach is to take action which provokes authorities into disclosing information about concealed activities, thus forcing a public debate on the principles and policies. Increasingly over the last twenty years this has been a favoured strategy by many non-governmental organisations (NGOs) with prosecutions leading to court cases which offer a public forum for an argued challenge to government policy. An example of this has been trespassing on military bases, as happened at Menwith Hill, and symbolically damaging or defacing bomber aircrafts, as carried out by the Trident Ploughshares campaign in Scotland. Current examples that are the subject of legal action are the open and reasoned refusal to pay taxes which will be used for military purposes, and the refusal to complete the census of 2011 on the grounds that the body carrying out the census is a private US company which is also linked to the manufacture of arms.

As the analysis of CAAB activities progresses it will become clear that the roots of the campaign lie partly in this tradition of non-violent action, and that it has maintained links with other groups in the UK which employ the full range of these methods. At the same time it acknowledges both the structural causes of violence and the personal responsibility to challenge violent solutions to problems and to develop alternative solutions and ways of thinking.

Civil liberties in Britain: The background

British people have long defined themselves as having a particular relationship with liberty and freedom, seeing modern liberty as in many ways Britain's unique contribution to politics and society. E.P.Thompson[10] argued that 'the belief that Britain was a country of liberty was more important than the reality'.

A brief overview of 'how liberty was won' in Britain is important in illuminating this aspect of CAAB's work, and places the campaign firmly in a radical tradition of protecting liberty in the face of state power, entering 'the battles (which) have to be fought by each generation'[11]. The battle is being fought in the context of a period when it is argued that 'the legislation affecting civil liberties enacted since 1997 is wide ranging and unprecedented in scale... the state has whittled away many of the rights we thought we could take for granted'[12].

What do we mean by 'civil liberties'? It is useful to distinguish them from the theory of Human Rights. Civil liberties are part of the contract between a state and its citizens. They vary from country to country and aim at a balance between individuals and the needs of society, especially in the areas of protection against crime, violence, invasion or health epidemics. In Britain they are enshrined in Common Law and Statute Law. The details of the challenges made by CAAB via the English legal system to the protection of civil liberties are explored in detail in Chapter 4, but it important to clarify the historical and political context in which they are located. Wilson[13] focussed on 'the value of history in explaining and defining liberty... the way in which society accommodates itself to contradictions, establishing a narrative of liberty'. Wilson's broad overview of the way in which liberty has established itself and been defined throughout British history from the seventeenth century to the present day yielded some unexpected insights and conclusions that contextualise and explain many of the legal and political processes encountered during the campaign. Wilson argued that, in Britain, in the absence of a written declaration of constitutional rights, it was left to the people to find and preserve what liberties they could. A central theme of Wilson's argument was that throughout British history, the state, has never granted liberties either willingly or through principle. Liberties have been wrested, bit by bit, by individual citizens. 'Liberty only found existence in the daily unremitting struggle of the citizen, not as passive recipients of whatever rights a ruler gives you'. 'It requires people to provoke power'[14]. E.P. Thompson believed that in Britain, this struggle is aided by what he calls 'a very ancient tradition of bloody-mindedness towards the intrusion of authority'[15].

Gearty[16] adopted a more inclusive approach to the history of civil liberties in Britain. He suggested that there are two opposing narratives at work here. Much civil libertarian protest takes place separately from parliamentary protest and draws strength from the belief that Parliament is irredeemably corrupted by power and wealth. There is therefore no alternative to protest. Mainstream politicians, by contrast, argue that our democratic system makes it unnecessary. He argued that the law and practice of civil liberties must take a principled stance between these two poles, and demonstrated (see later Chapter 4) that an examination of civil liberties legislation in the twentieth century contradicts to some extent both these polarised views. He argued that our belief in civil liberties and political freedom is currently placed under strain by international terrorism, globalisation and environmental degradation.

Wilson described in detail the impact in twentieth century Britain of the two world wars on the history of civil liberties, a story that has resonances for the period after the attacks on the Twin Towers in New York on September 11 2001, commonly known there-after as 9/11. During World War 1 the Defence of the Realm Act (DORA) (1914), gave powers to the state over every aspect of civilian life, and effectively removed the powers of parliament. Nor did these extraordinary powers cease in 1918, but were re-invoked to deal with the General Strike of 1926 and the serious civil unrest in the 1930s. Significantly, parliament largely failed to act as the watchdog of liberty. Laski[17] called the years of 1914 to 1951 'the twilight world' when Britain provided, in his view, a 'stark vision of what happens when civil liberties go unregarded'. In many instances the government turned to old laws, particularly those dating from the war years of the 1810s and 1820s to justify their actions in law.

17

Gearty noted that the retention and transfer into ordinary law, of emergency measures passed during World War 1, was justified on the grounds of the perceived threat of the recent revolution in Russia, of the commitment of the new USSR to export that revolution, and the perceived threat of the newly formed Communist Party in Britain. Civil Libertarian protest during the 1920s and 1930s was not over the principle of speech control but rather the ways in which the authorities used their power, for example in banning hunger marches and communist rallies while turning a benign eye on Fascist demonstrations. This continued after World War 2 when the dominance of perceived Communist threats led to a wide range of truncations to civil liberties. He believed that this was a widely accepted compromise between civil liberties and the state's commitment to maintain security and freedom, and that senior judges were invariably supportive of this. Gearty perceived a change in these judicial attitudes which he thinks may have been partly due to a succession of miscarriages of justice in the 1970s and 1980s, and partly to the difference in backgrounds of judges on the bench, which made them more responsive to public perceptions.

Wilson argued that the real language of freedom during the twentieth century belonged to 'outsiders' and people on the left of politics who regarded themselves as the true heirs of the radical inheritance, while the ruling class backed away. He repeated that battles have to be fought anew by each generation and argued, controversially, that it is the long historical tradition of freedom and individual liberty that has, over the centuries, provided a better bulwark than laws and constitutions. 'Shouting from the roof tops every time a minor infraction of liberty was suspected kept a country free, even if it looked somewhat paranoid', and 'individuals who have pursued through the courts the process of finding barriers against authority have not been sufficiently celebrated'[18].

The Campaign for the Accountability of American bases has been conducted mainly during the 1990s and 2000s, years of the last Conservative government of the twentieth century, of the 13 years of the New Labour Government and, at the time of writing, of a Coalition Government. There has developed during these years a serious critique of the threats to civil liberties in Britain grounded in not only post 9/11 fears of terrorism but also in what Wilson called 'the New Orthodoxy'. Wilson meant by this term the development during the last 30 years of acceptance of a radically changed view of the role of the state, with lower and middle tiers of government eroded so that functions have been transferred either to Whitehall or to private contractors. He questioned the assumption that liberty has increasingly been seen as leading to excessive individualism so that the protection of individual rights is seen as less important than the effective administration of justice and the protection of the public interest. The then Prime Minister, Tony Blair expressed the view that 'Civil Liberties were invented for another age'. Wilson argued that increasingly the old protections against injustice have been removed in the name of efficiency, and that there has developed fear of, and collapse in, the laws and institutions that made us free. He lists the Acts of Parliament passed in the years of New Labour, and analyses their implications for civil liberties in Britain. The discussion of these acts is left to Chapters 4 and 5, where CAAB's campaigning activities provide examples of the working of these acts and in particular their impact on peaceful protest.

Judt[19], in an analysis of the last 30 years in Britain, argued that what appears 'natural' in our society today actually dates from the 1980s. 'The obsession with wealth creation, the cult of privatisation and the private sector, the growing disparities between rich and poor', are, after the financial crash of 2008, no longer sustainable and require a new alternative, 'the urgency of a return to an ethically informed public conversation'.[20] Wilson argued that, in the context of 9/11, 'we have given up too many freedoms in order to be free' and need to begin to struggle with difficult issues about the role of the state, moving from what he calls the 'ideological bankruptcy of politics'[21].

Sampson[22] in his study of the institutions of Britain and in a quest for an answer to his core question 'Who runs this place?' argued that in the particular area of national security, with which CAAB was particularly concerned, Britain's internal security services have since 9/11 become more intrusive in everyday activity. He also examined the role of MI6, the key intelligence agency in international affairs, noted its expanded budget and staff, and of particular relevance to the CAAB campaign, its relationship with GCHQ, the massive electronic system at Cheltenham, and its crucial cooperation with the US National Security Agency. Sampson referred back to the Hutton Enquiry of 2003 and its revelations of a network of intelligence agencies of which the public is unaware. More importantly, this enquiry revealed the dangers of the politicisation of these services leading to distortions of the truth, and contributing to difficulties in exercising democratic control. A key example of the evasion of democratic control over an intelligence agency came in 2003. A British Intelligence officer, Katherine Gunn, working at GCHQ in the run up to the invasion of Iraq in 2003, saw an email from a senior NSA officer requesting support in covert surveillance members of the United Nations Security Council to gain leverage over their votes concerning the legality of the invasion. She leaked the email advising this illegal activity to the Observer newspaper and was prosecuted under the Official secrets Act; her trial later collapsed when the British Government withdrew its charges since a trial would have exposed confidential legal opinions on the legality of the decision to go to war.

This brief overview aims at enabling the reader to understand the principles behind the many court challenges undertaken by CAAB, demonstrates how its concerns were particularly relevant to a time of real social and political change, and shows how it could contribute to a positive and forward looking debate on fundamental questions posed by both Wilson and Judt:

'How do we contribute to a robust defence of the principles of freedom and of British values, of the basic liberties we have built up, at great cost over the last 500 years? How do we teach the universal rules of freedom, and what are the dangers of cutting ourselves off from this tradition?'

The Quaker connection

This section sets out to explore what is distinctively Quaker about CAAB in terms of its values, methods and structure. The following overview of the 'Quaker connection' will include for non-Quaker readers, an explanation of any

21

unusual terms used. Both campaigners describe their work as strongly rooted in Quaker values and as inspired by the historic Quaker testimonies. To use a Quaker term, they are acting 'under concern'.

'Throughout the history of the Religious Society of Friends we have recognised that to anyone may come, at any special time a 'special inward calling to carry out a particular service[23]. 'A concern may arise unexpectedly out of an interest or may creep up on one... it may be in line with current desires and projects or it may cut across them; it may lead to action which is similar to that undertaken by others or it may require a brave striking out into the unknown[24]. Historically, ministry which is carried out under concern, such Elizabeth Fry's work in prisons, or the challenge by John Woolman to the owning of slaves in America, is 'remarkable as a record of strength and perseverance in adversity'[25].

It is useful at this point therefore to locate the campaign in the context of Quaker peace work since the founding of the Religious Society of Friends in the mid seventeenth century. This brief overview is not simply of historical interest; it examines not only its achievements, but also the criticism which it has at times attracted, and the dilemmas and issues which became apparent. Of the four historic testimonies of Friends, three are of particular relevance. By way of explanation, a testimony is not a creed, test or belief, to be used as a sign of membership, but 'actions and words intended to demonstrate and convince', 'a form of communication to the whole world... a witness to a personally experienced truth'[26]. 'Testimonies are not imposed on members of the Society of Friends but... are both a challenge and a way of living for most Friends. They are part of our distinctive witness'[27].

The historic Peace Testimony is possibly the one for which Quakers are most widely known, the one which is most easily identified, but also the one most easily equated with a simplistic definition of pacifism that is based on a naive conceptualisation of violence and conflict and how they may be addressed. In fact the history of Quakers and peace shows a different and more complex range of activities in response to the profound changes in societies in the last 350 years. The earliest statement of Friends' testimony against war is contained in the declaration to Charles the Second in 1660, which sets out the basic principles and at the same time aims to distinguish Quakers from those plotting to overthrow the establishment. It declared:

'All bloody principles and practices we do utterly deny with all outward wars, and strife, and fightings with outward weapons, for any end, or with any pretence whatsoever, and this is our testimony to the whole world'[28].

Over the following centuries, formal statements set out Friends' reiteration of the testimony, in the context of different wars; the Napoleonic wars (1804/6), the South African Wars (1900), and during two world wars (1915 and 1943). This statement of principle did not evade the dilemmas of the pacifist stand. Isaac Pennington, writing in 1661 added to his witness against war a caveat which still contains a challenge to non-violent principles. 'I speak not against any magistrate or peoples defending themselves

23

against foreign invasions; or making use of the sword to suppress the violent and evil-doers within their borders'[(29)]. In 1949, speaking about his service in the second world war wrote, Roger Wilson wrote 'I do not think it was possible to contemplate coming to any sort of political compromise with (the Nazi philosophy) and speaking as a Christian pacifist I had a far deeper spiritual unity with those of my friends in the fighting services... than with those pacifists who talked as if the suffering of the world could be turned off like a water tap if only the politicians would talk sensibly together'[(30)].

The Testimony to Equality among early Friends has its roots in the radical political debates of the seventeenth century about the structure of society which flourished briefly among such groups as the Levellers and Diggers who, with their vision of 'a world turned upside down' and of radical changes in the distribution of land and wealth, incurred a savage response during the Commonwealth and following the restoration of Charles the Second. Early Friends witnessed against the rigidly defined social distinctions of seventeenth century England, challenging language which emphasised hierarchy (hence the use of 'thee' and 'thou', commonly used to address social 'inferiors' and children instead of the more formal 'you'), and the refusal to doff hats as a sign of deference. This witness inspired John Woolman (1720-1772), an American Quaker who was the first Friend to voice a reasoned and principled opposition to the owning of slaves, to write, when asked by a neighbour to write down his will: 'He told me to which of his children he gave his young negro: I wrote his will, save only that part concerning his slave... and told him I could not write any instrument by which my fellow-creatures were made slaves'[31]. The testimony to equality developed into a statement that is not just about individual behaviour but applies to the distribution of wealth, to our attitude to life as a whole and to our behaviour towards human beings be they slaves, prisoners, children working in sweat shops world-wide, girls forced into marriage while little more than children, or victims of torture. 'At the centre...is the consistently expressed belief in the fundamental equality of all members of the human race. Our common humanity transcends our differences'[32].

The Testimony to Truth. Early Friends witnessed to the truth by continuing to hold public Meetings for Worship despite severe persecution and legal penalties, by refusing to take public oaths since this implied a double standard of truth, and also by using 'plainness of both habit and speech'[33]. From this testimony has arisen the concern not only for truth and integrity in our day to day relationships, personal and business, but also in public affairs. Thus in 1987, Cecil Evans[34] wrote: 'Our primary objective in speaking truth to power on social and economic issues, especially on the problem of world poverty should be in the interests of the poor'. And in 1989 a conference held by Warwick Area Meeting (the local Quaker Meeting for business affairs) reported that 'what we have heard on the degree of secrecy which permeates our national institutions brings out in us fear, shock, distress and dilemma at the level of deviousness and distortion that flows from this. We need to uphold those who experience persecution and harassment as a result of this secrecy[35].

2011 marked the 350th anniversary of the 1661 Peace Declaration. Quakers used the occasion to examine in 'The

Friend' and other Quaker Journals some of the dilemmas of building peace in the twenty- first century. They noted that the Quaker reputation for peace continued to be one of the Society's most well known characteristics', but that the emphasis increasingly is on dealing with the 'roots of unpeacefulness'. Some dilemmas are explored, for example, 'what is a peaceful response to terrorism?', 'how do we sustain humility... and resist the natural ego temptations in working at this level?', and, going back to first principles, 'how do we view the assertion of Isaac Penington that 'a great blessing may attend the sword where it is born uprightly to that end' (the 'suppression of violence and evil doers') and 'its use will be honourable'? The work of Quaker Peace and Social Witness (QPSW) was also described, detailing the activities of 27 staff, working from Friends' House in London, who are engaged in a wide range of peace work including conciliation, training in non violence, and supporting Friends engaged in non-violent protest. Of particular relevance to CAAB, Steve Whitling[36] noted that in relation to the breadth of Quaker work outlined in this review 'resistance work is a very poor relation; non-violent action is often uncomfortable, involves confrontation and demands sacrifice'. He argued that in Britain now, the 'legal space' for resistance is being reduced, as the accounts of the CAAB campaigners' experience have indicated, and that there has to be concern about the role, attitude and culture of the police in managing protest. In the same issue, Sam Walton describing his work with QPSW, which included monitoring what the police are doing and offering advice to non-violent protestors, voiced genuine concern about repressive policing of non-violent protests and asked how

Friends are responding to this. This aspect of the work of a central committee of Friends House suggests that it is close in principle and practice to one of the key concerns of CAAB, and as has already been noted, echoes the experience of other protest campaigns. In all the discussions on the 350th Peace Testimony anniversary conducted in the pages of 'The Friend' in 2011, there is a real awareness of the hard reality of non-violent protest which was voiced by Wolf Mendel in 1974:

'The failure to take evil and conflict into account as elements of our human condition and an obsession with the need for peace and harmony have led pacifists badly astray... Christian pacifists (are) not exempt from the temptation to sacrifice others for the sake of peace'[37]

It is important that the above account of the engagement by the Society of Friends in work relating to peace, social justice, truthfulness and integrity in personal and public affairs, does not convey the impression that Friends were and are unique in these values and activities. Quakers have maintained a sustained witness against war and have also consistently shown the ability to work with peace groups who do not regard all war as evil. While taking an active part in the nineteenth century peace movement, rooted in the Evangelical revival and the Enlightenment, Quakers were prepared to argue on pragmatic grounds against the dangers, financial cost and destructiveness of war. Similarly, in the anti-slavery campaign Friends worked with campaigners from a wide spectrum of religious and political convictions. This pragmatism is also demonstrated in the ability of CAAB to work with groups such as CND, Liberty, and mainstream churches who share many of the aims and values of CAAB without necessarily sharing its underlying commitment to non-violence.

In 2002 CAAB, together with two Quaker groups, Northern Friends Peace Board (NFPB) and Quaker Peace and Service (QSP,) joined together with five other organisations, CND, the Campaign against the Arms Trade (CAT), Abolition 2000, and UNA-UK, and Medact to focus on the proposed use of US bases in the UK as part of the US Missile Defense system (American spelling is used here since it describes an American military system) Their report (pub. 2004) outlined the danger of this strategy for both US/Russia relations, for international peace and security and particularly for the UK. In relation to the latter they pointed to the danger that US bases would 'raise the profile of the UK in any missile attack on the UK'[38]. It also endorsed concern about the 'opaque operation of US bases in the UK' and about the 'lack of parliamentary debate (which) raises questions of UK sovereignty in respect of these bases and their overall accountability'. It raised the issue of the risks to health and the environment in the UK from Weapons of Mass Destruction (WMD) exploding over Europe, a risk that has not been investigated. In broader terms the report presented a 10 point critique of US Missile Defense (USMD), including the weaponisation of space, concluding with the argument that the resources devoted to this programme could be used to 'address the systemic causes of insecurity to better effect. The report concluded by summarising the key arguments against involvement in a USMD system, but also suggested reasonable alternatives to securing international peace in which the UK is seen as well placed to take the leadership in providing diplomatic engagement. In particular they argued that the issue is one of serious public concern and one which merits open public and parliamentary debate.

Present day Friends are aware of the dilemmas and challenges of a peace witness at the start of the twenty-first century, of living out values which are at odds with mainstream society and of being part of the fabric of society without being compromised. In the nineteenth century Friends had a membership made largely of manufacturers, bankers, and business and trade people since they were excluded from the professions and higher education. They were not apart from society and, in Pennsylvania and Rhode Island, American Quakers had the experience of grappling with the reality of government and the legitimacy of the use of force in civil situations. Indeed, a Quaker historian, Hirst[39] noted that Quakers were, at the end of the nineteenth century and during World War One, accused of complacency about their place in society, and of being too anxious about the possible effects of civil unrest. In the eighteenth century many Quakers in the Americas had been relatively comfortable about slave ownership until challenged by John Woolman.

The Society of Friends in Britain had 14,345 in membership in 2010, mainly white, and from middle class and professional backgrounds. It also, like many other faith groups, has an aging membership. These distinctive characteristics may mean that less energy is available for serious involvement in political struggles that are both personally and financially

29

costly, as the CAAB campaign has shown them to be. One critic of Britain Yearly Meeting (the annual gathering of all Friends in Britain) in 2010 asked why, at a time when Britain had soldiers in Afghanistan in a costly and unpopular war, the issue was not on the agenda[40]. David Bolton argued that Friends are in danger of priding themselves on their absolute principle of non-violence without seriously grappling with the spiritual depth and clear-sightedness needed to be a genuine pacifist, or even with fundamental questions such as whether we can be peacemakers without being pacifists[41].

This is not to ignore the breadth of Quaker-supported concerns and initiatives in some key twentieth-century conflicts, such as reconstruction in post-war Germany, building bridges between east and west in Europe during the cold war, in Nigeria, the Indian sub-continent, in Northern Ireland and South Africa, maintaining a presence at the United Nations and in Brussels at the heart of the European Community. Friends' House in London, through the work of one of its central committees Quaker Peace and Social Witness (QPSW), has also helped Friends, both individually and corporately, to look at current conflicts and the controversies and dilemmas which arise from them, and to examine how Quakers respond to them in the light of the Society's experience over the last 300 years. This examination has encouraged Friends to look not only at international conflicts but also at local and community issues and at the creation of peace in our daily lives. Friends were the prime movers in establishing the first Chair in Peace Studies at the University of Bradford which has pioneered academic research and teaching in these areas.

These considerations go some way to helping us with some key issues about peace campaigning in general and CAAB in particular. Any reader of the CAAB records will be struck by the way in which the campaigners were continually drawn into new and challenging areas of campaigning and of witness: the detail of nuclear and space weaponry, the institutions of government, the law and the functioning of the courts, prison conditions especially in relation to women, relations with the police and the public, and the frightening and unpredictable encounters with physical violence. Wolf Mendel[42] noted that 'the emphasis on personal action... inevitably raises the question of where one draws the line. There are no formal rules laid down for Quaker conduct in such circumstances, other than to follow the Light...' At times the personal and ethical dilemmas are stark. There is evidence of the importance of the support for CAAB from local Quaker meetings, and of real personal and financial support from individual Friends as well as from other peace campaigners. There remains a key question of what impact a more structured and formal organisation would have had on this small and personally cohesive campaign. Views from independent evaluators on the effectiveness of the campaign are described in Chapter 6.

It is useful also to include some warning voices about the limits and inherent problems of principled non violent action which underpins much of CAAB's work. Yarrow[43] noted that the Quaker faith is that 'a concern has its own justification in the light of eternity', but adds that such views, valid and unassailable in their own right, cut no ice with social scientists and 'can be an excuse for muddled thinking, less than rigorous practice and wasted resources'.

Phillips[44] urged Friends not to 'mistake access for real influence' or to be caught up in 'a seductive and unrealistic vision of Quakers as having a historic destiny at the heart of the nation's affairs'. The positive and professional reactions to the campaign from interviewees discussed in Chapter 6 suggest that CAAB has a more focussed and rigorous approach than this, but the questions are important ones and deserve research and informed evaluation.

CAAB cannot, in strict terms, be described as a Quaker concern. There is a clear procedure which Friends with a particular concern are encouraged to adopt. The individual is advised to 'take counsel from experienced members of the Meeting, particularly those with a different approach to the problem'[45], to consider 'setting up a support group of trusted Friends' and to allow for a 'Meeting for Clearness to be part of the process of discernment'. After a period of questioning and elucidation, the local Area Meeting will decide whether to support the Friend in his or her concern, who is then given a minute (in Quaker terminology 'a statement of record') to take the matter forward, giving attention to the practical details of implementation and contingencies. Financial responsibility may be assumed by the Meeting and, if it relates clearly to the corporate life of Britain Yearly Meeting (BYM), will be sent to this body. Emphasis is laid on the importance of support for the individual and for the ongoing consideration of when a concern has run its course and may be laid down.

This detailed account of Quaker practice clearly shows both the time and rigour devoted to testing a concern, and to ongoing support for the individuals who carry the spiritual, personal and financial costs of the service. It is obvious from the records that the campaigners, who are respectively a Member and Attender at local Meetings, did not choose to go down this path. This should not be seen as necessarily an unusual choice. Sydney Bailey[46] distinguished Quaker Service organised from Friends' House from 'Service by Quakers' and noted that for two centuries there was no standing committee at London Yearly Meeting for relief abroad, which was carried out by individual Friends 'acting under concern'. It is important to be clear that many Friends work for organisations such as Amnesty, Liberty or the UN which are not Quaker organisations, but which Friends feel allow them to put their testimonies into practice. This presents relevant and searching questions to Friends which would both encourage clarity about the advantages to Quaker campaigners of taking a concern through Quaker procedures, and whether there would have been any such advantages for CAAB.

Chapter 3

US Bases in Britain: The importance of Menwith Hill

It is difficult to understand the thinking and conviction behind CAAB without an introduction to US foreign policy after World War 2, with particular attention given to the period after the ending of the Cold War in the early 1990s, and the rapid and revolutionary advances in technology which transformed intelligence-led warfare. This analysis leads into an examination of Britain's role in US global strategy and in particular the importance of the continually expanding base at Menwith Hill in Yorkshire. The sources for this chapter are the bulk of written documentation built up by the campaign workers during the campaign, in addition to the web-site material. This documentation covers defence and military issues gathered from publicly accessible websites and information amassed by investigative journalists. These subjects are summarised in regular information papers published by the campaign, which elucidate the key issues on a particular topic, and incidentally demonstrate how much time was devoted to amassing information from a variety of sources and then exposing their limitations in the light of the research activities and court cases carried out by CAAB. Wherever possible, an attempt will be made to separate *process* from *findings* so that readers can distinguish the *methods* of the campaigners, from *what they found out.* Reference is also made to a Yorkshire CND publication of 2012, 'Lifting the lid on Menwith Hill',[47] which is particularly valuable for an analysis of operational and command structures at Menwith Hill, and for a critical assessment of the evidence for the economic value to the local community of having a US base in North Yorkshire.

One of the most striking findings from perusal of the CAAB records is the tenacity and thoroughness with which information on key issues is pursued. Methods of gaining information include the sharing of information between researchers, academics investigative journalists, peace activists and other campaigners both in the UK and world-wide. In a 'Guardian' article of 4/2/99 Diane Taylor noted that 'the modern peace campaigner is more likely to spend her time poring over technical military information', and in a later article of 5/4/2000, Richard Norton-Taylor, an investigative journalist in defence and security matters for the 'Guardian' specifically refers to the role of Lindis Percy in uncovering the status of US bases in Britain, and the reality of who controls what is done there. In particular he says that the most significant document gained by her was the paper signed by a senior official in the Treasury, releasing the text of the agreement signed by the British Government which governs the legal status of the bases, admitting that the RAF commanders have no right to interfere with anything that the Americans do on the bases and stating that 'the Americans will, in fact, be in sole occupation'. In February

1992, an Early Day Motion in the House of Commons, signed by 14 MPs, praised the work of CAAB and urged it to continue its campaign to provide public information about 'this unwarranted establishment' (ie. Menwith Hill).

The background of US post war military strategy

US bases in Britain (of which a fuller analysis follows in this chapter), are only part of a world-wide network. Since the end of World War 2 one of the prime concerns of US foreign and military policy was the safeguarding of access to oil and other raw materials, the supply of which underpinned its industrial and military dominance. In particular, the Persian Gulf region became vital to US economic and national security interests, as well as the safeguarding of transportation routes for tankers and pipe lines. The Cold War, with the perceived threat of global communism, enhanced the arguments for a world wide spread of US bases and, some would argue, the development of a policy of US support for often corrupt and usually anti-democratic regimes which supported US economic interests. By the beginning of the 1990s there were over 1000 US bases world-wide, ranging from large establishments with over 20,000 personnel to small radar stations. (For a more detailed description of this see the Yorkshire CND report of 2012.) With the end of the Cold War it would have been reasonable to expect that many of these bases would be closed, with a reduction in military spending, and even with nuclear disarmament within the decade. Instead, a new wave of base establishments began, but on the basis of different defence thinking, and the understanding of this change is most important in assessing the growing importance of Menwith Hill

During the 1960s and 1970s the emphasis was now to utilise revolutionary changes in technology to establish a world- wide network of communication systems, using the developing space-based satellites, to provide information for the US military. In effect this would provide a system of communication and information networks that would increase the speed and accuracy of US military deployments. The military and diplomatic situation was changed fundamentally by the events of 9/11. The threat to the US and to its allies could now arguably be seen as international terrorism, which justified further the development of intercepting not only military intelligence but also private electronic communications. During the early 2000s the US arms budget under President Bush rose from \$290 billion to \$380 billion, a development based on arguments that significant changes world-wide justify this increase. The most notable of these are the growing demand from China and India for oil and other raw materials to meet their growing manufacturing industries, and the anticipated long-term decline in oil production from the Persian Gulf, thus requiring the US to identify major new sources of oil, such as the Caspian Sea region, with the accompanying need to secure routes through India and Pakistan.

This huge development of world-wide communications networks cannot be understood without reviewing the importance of the US National Security Agency (NSA) which, as will be shown later, controls the base at Menwith Hill. The NSA was established in 1952, with its structure and funding classified as top secret. By the mid 1950s it employed 4000 staff, with its HQ at Fort Meade in Maryland. Its priority was research and development of high-speed computers for code breaking and for the transfer, analysis and storage of data generated by its listening posts overseas. During the 1960s and 1970s the US devoted resources to the development of a space-based system of intelligence which came from military spy satellites. Each satellite covered a major region thus giving coverage of the entire planet, and their communications would be directed to ground-based station for analysis and dispatch to Fort Meade. By 2007, the NSA's budget was an estimated $10 billion a year, and the staff at Fort Meade exceeded 50,000.

An important parallel development in US defence strategy, and one which was to be of importance to Menwith Hill as will be seen later, was the plan to use the new Space Based Infra Red System (SBIRS) to detect the launch of ballistic missiles, and convey this information to the US Space Command Center (again American spelling is used), which would then have the capability to destroy them in flight. There are doubts about whether this system is of proven effectiveness, but it is obvious that such a development would have far-reaching implications. Although it could be justified as effective against 'rogue states' it could also be directed against major powers such as China or Russia, and might be perceived by such powers as a first strike capability for nuclear attack, and thus in effect destabilising existing agreements on the use of ballistic missiles.

Britain, the US and Menwith Hill

Against this background it is now possible to examine the part that Britain has played in international strategy since WW2, and in particular in its relationship with the US.

Britain has long had a close relationship with the US in intelligence gathering. The importance of signals intelligence (SIGINT) was already recognised when the two countries worked together at Bletchley Park, intercepting German and Japanese electronic communications. This centre was later transferred to Government Communications headquarters at Cheltenham (GCHQ), which used an exclusive network of interception facilities, including HMS Forest Moor near Harrogate in Yorkshire, and other stations in the UK and world-wide. As early as 1948, Britain and the US signed an intelligence treaty, later including Canada, Australia and New Zealand, which established reciprocity in sharing intelligence. The reality of the relationship, certainly as far as Britain is concerned, is that it early became clear that only the US had the money and technological resources to develop spy satellites and in the 1970s Britain abandoned any attempts to develop its own. Instead Britain invested in a share of the new satellites and developed an important role in NSA monitoring, based on GCHQ, Menwith Hill and Morwenstow in Cornwall. This goes at least some way to providing an understanding of the repeated statements by successive British governments of the importance attached to intelligence- sharing with the US. It also contributes to our understanding of the analysis in this chapter of US bases in Britain, and the secrecy and disinformation that surround them.

It will be argued that during the last 50 years, and particularly since the early 1990s, Menwith Hill has occupied a significant strategic role in US defence, particularly in its contribution to NSA's global network of systems intelligence, its role in the US Ballistic Missile Defence Programme (BMD), and currently as a key regional centre for intercepting and integrating telecommunications and satellite imagery, which is relayed to the US to support their military operations. CAAB demonstrated repeatedly that during these years successive UK governments complied with this expansion and specialisation, without any public or parliamentary discussion, and with no insistence on democratic oversight.

In 2013, an ex-employee of NSA, Edward Snowden, leaked to the media a series of documents showing the unprecedented reach of electronic surveillance by NSA and its British counterpart, GCHQ. The data showed that the two agencies have been harvesting the personal data of citizens and listening to the electronic communications of world leaders, including those of 'friendly countries' such as Germany and Spain. These documents were, after redaction of part of the information on grounds of potential security harm, then published by the New York Times and the Guardian newspapers. The publication prompted serious and sometimes furious debate world-wide. Most of the revelations were not surprising to CAAB and to other organisations in Britain who had for years been alerting the public to the dangers of such surveillance. The presence at Menwith Hill, NSA's surveillance hub in Europe, of numbers of GCHQ staff (figures withheld on 'grounds of security') have suggested close collaboration between the two bodies, and therefore the likelihood that the base has been used for the known instances of spying on foreign leaders. In 'The Guardian, of 15/10/2013, Snowden's documents show that the base was used for intercepting the secret electronic communications President Medvedev of Russia when he attended, in 2009, the G20 summit in Britain. This was then shared with Canada, New Zealand and Australia. GCHQ is also revealed to be proud of the relative laxity of legal oversight of its activities compared with the US. A further development which illustrates the close and secret relationship between the US and Britain in intelligence sharing, is the revelation, published in the Guardian newspaper on 21/11/2013 of a memo of 2007 which showed a secret agreement giving the US the right of access to personal data on British citizens not suspected of any crimes.

The terms of public debate which have developed in Britain after these revelations are strikingly similar to those raised by CAAB throughout its years of campaigning. What are the terms of these secret agreements between the UK and the US? Were they ever debated in Parliament? What is the nature of democratic oversight of the activities of these agencies? A former Conservative Home Office minister, Lord Blencathra, has expressed anger that when his committee enquired into the Communications Data Bill of 2009 (later abandoned by the Coalition) they were never told of GCHQ's surveillance capabilities. He expressed strong reservations about the Tempora Programme which allows GCHQ to harvest, store and analyse millions of calls, emails and enquiries to search engines, by tapping transatlantic cables and sharing the data with the US. He says that his committee was not told of this programme and asks whether the British public ever consented to this.

Fundamental questions are now being raised which go to the heart of parliamentary democracy and civil liberties in Britain. What are the borderlines between national security and democratic transparency? Who should oversee the activities of intelligence agencies who now have the ability, unprecedented in history, to pry into millions of lives? Were the surveillance agreements between the US and the UK publicly debated and authorised by Parliament? Does the sharing of intelligence lie at the heart of the 'Special Relationship' and where is the public discussion of the advantages and disadvantages of this in a changing world? Why has debate about the revelations been more muted and equivocal in Britain than in the US and Europe? And, importantly, what are the responsibilities of journalists in revealing to their countries' citizens information about what their governments are doing in areas hitherto kept secret?

This challenge to government secrecy, to dividing lines between security and democratic accountability, and to issues of national sovereignty, are questions which CAAB has been exposing and developing during its years of campaigning.

If we want to understand the nature of the expansion at Menwith Hill, the following figures are highly significant (they are drawn from the Yorkshire CND publication 2012, noted above). By 1960, when it was fully operational as an NSA base, it had around 400 US personnel. By 1980 this had risen to 850 US personnel plus 340 US staff in military and support roles. These figures exclude GCHQ staff who were seconded there, but not numbered in the official information 'for security reasons'. By the end of the 1990's, there were 1370 US military and civilian personnel, with 390 UK support staff. By 2007 this had risen further to 1410 US and 433 UK personnel. Figures from the US Department of Defense give a planned increase of service personnel to 2,300 by 2015, when the base becomes fully functional as a US Regional Security Operations Centre. The radomes have shown a similar exponential increase in numbers from the first in 1974 to 26 by the end of the 1990's. Currently the number of radomes at Menwith Hill is 33. What does Menwith Hill provide that makes this rapid expansion so necessary to the US? In the context of US military and commercial strategies outlined earlier in this chapter it is clear that Menwith Hill makes an important contribution in three main areas.

First, as a major receiving centre for communications from spy satellites and commercial satellites. Menwith Hill is the main regional centre covering Europe and the former Warsaw pact countries, and is responsible for analysing and transmitting this information to Fort Meade. Secondly, during the 1990s Menwith Hill expanded due to the increased responsibility for downloading information from military satellites covering the Persian Gulf region thus giving it a key role during the first Gulf War, for which it gained a US award. During the 1990s it also saw a growth in its capacity for intercepting ground- based telecommunications, particularly via fibre optic cables, connected into British Telecom's tele-communications network, for covering UK and internal communications. Thirdly, it has a key role in the SBIRS programme. Menwith

Hill is a key ground relay station, linking the new SBIRS satellites to the USAF Space Communications Centre. It is argued that this major escalation in the militarisation of space increases significantly the chance of a new arms race and breaches the missile treaty between the US and Russia. Menwith Hill is currently undergoing a major construction programme to provide accommodation for advanced computer hardware and software to deal with the massive increase in communication. The base now provides surveillance to support US military operations in the region for which it is responsible. It is the designated Regional Security Operations Centre for Europe, North Africa, the Middle East and the Indian Ocean.

What follows is a detailed analysis of CAAB's activities in exposing not only key developments at Menwith Hill but also the danger to democratic and accountable government, and to national sovereignty, revealed by the process by which the continued expansion was allowed, and the ongoing dangers posed by the base's continued presence and ways of functioning. It is important to stress also the importance of early research work by independent analysts such as the US author, James Bamford, and Duncan Campbell, a British investigative journalist. Throughout the 1970s and 1980s Campbell contributed, by a series of articles in the New Statesman, followed by a TV programme, to a critical understanding of the role of Menwith Hill, and in subsequent publications[48] developed a wider analysis of US intelligence activities in Britain.

As a brief background, it is known that there have been US bases in the UK since 1941, and that from these origins the presence of the USAF has been maintained to the present day. After the formation of NATO in 1945, it was decided that the USAF would restore a larger presence, with a major expansion of bases, particularly in East Anglia, to accommodate jet aircraft under Strategic Air Command. The bases in the UK are governed by the terms of the NATO agreement of 1951 and other confidential agreements between the two governments. Officially, these bases have RAF Commanders, who act as liaison officers. CAAB's argument over the years of their campaigning has been that official information about what actually happens on these bases has been often incomplete and sometimes with held or inaccurate, hence the focus of CAAB on the steady questioning and search for information which has focussed a revealing spotlight on the US bases.

Menwith Hill was established in 1951 with land purchased under compulsory order from local farmers, and the original agreement was that it would be a US army base. In 1996, the NSA took it over from the US army and it was officially renamed as an RAF base with an RAF flag and a nominal RAF Commander. Many British citizens are puzzled and surprised to hear of the presence of US bases in Britain. In part this is because they are called RAF bases, a designation which was always intended to hide the extent of the US presence in Britain. It is not difficult to access information on these bases from official websites. At the time of writing (2012) there are 10 US bases at: Menwith Hill, Fylingdales (North Yorkshire), Lakenheath, Mildenhall and Molesworth (Cambridgeshire), Croughton / Barford St. John (Northamptonshire), Fairford (Gloucestershire), Alconbury (Huntingdon), Feltwell (Norfolk) and Welford (Berkshire). From the early days, concern was expressed by local citizens in Yorkshire about the base at Menwith Hill, and there were protests at the base by local peace groups. Serious questions were asked. Who owns the base? Who controls it? What rights does parliament have over what happens there? Who pays? What would be its role in a nuclear war? What if the US wanted to use the base for weapons that the UK did not support? What powers would the UK government have over the use of the base in a conflict where US and UK foreign policies did not coincide? These questions are not the concerns of peace campaigners alone. They lead into issues of national sovereignty, of costs in a time of recession, and questions of whether being part of a US world-wide web of bases contributes to tensions between Britain and other countries, particularly with the Muslim world and in our own society.

CAAB'S campaigning methods

How did CAAB gain access to information about Menwith HIll, given the extreme secrecy which surrounds it? The records show a variety of methods of gaining access to information in an area shrouded by official secrecy.

1. Entering US bases

In 1990/91, Lindis Percy then subject to an injunction which barred her from entering Menwith Hill, worked with a campaigner from another local protest group, Anne Lee to enter the base and remove black bags of shredded and discarded information. Among the pizza trays and discarded food were original documents such as bills and a telephone list for the whole base. These and other documents were passed to the investigative journalist Duncan Campbell, and formed the basis of his 'Dispatches' documentary on Menwith Hill, shown on Channel 4. All the documents were returned before the programme was broadcast so that the campaigners could not be accused of theft.

2. Monitoring planning applications

At the local level the campaigners monitored, as did peace campaigners at other bases, planning applications and decisions which gave clues as to proposed changes in the bases. Thus, campaigners were the first to pick up from Harrogate Planning Office indications of a significant expansion of Menwith Hill in 1997, when planning permission was sought for two new giant radomes (plastic sheeting covering an aluminium frame which protects the receiving dishes), support buildings, roads and security fencing. The time involved in monitoring other US bases was beyond the resources of CAAB, and other local groups have not undertaken the consistent scrutiny which was so useful to CAAB. However the Oxford peace group together with the local CND are to undertake a similar task for RAF Croughton.

3. Asking questions in parliament

Requesting sympathetic MP's to table parliamentary questions which would require the relevant minister to give information on the floor of the House of Commons. In the CAAB records there are hundreds of carefully worded draft questions for such MPs to submit. This exercise in itself revealed what has since become apparent in the history of the events leading up to the Iraq war, that parliamentary control of, and access to, information about defence and security issues is severely limited. When the renewal of the 'Security of Tenure' agreement on MHS became due in 1997, questions about the terms of the agreement were tabled by, among others, the late Max Madden and Harold Best (both Yorkshire MPs), and in recent years by Norman Baker (who withdrew after taking office in the coalition government), Colin Challen and David Drew (Independent MP) succeeded by Fabian Hamilton. The response of the Secretary of State for Defence was that this information was 'confidential' and related to arrangements for US and UK defence. There are many examples of questions prepared by CAAB which aimed to clarify the function and operation of US bases in Britain, and where the response shows the secrecy surrounding them. The following are selected from CAAB reports during the years of the campaign.

Question: Will the MOD make public the cost sharing agreement between the US and UK governments regarding the cost of visiting forces?

Answer: 'This is confidential under exemption 1 of the Code of Practice on Access to Government Information'.

Question: Will the MOD make public what proportion of information collected at MHS is available to the British security Services?

Answer: as above

Question: What do we know about US interception of UK citizens' communications?

Answer: as above.

Question: Do US forces have chemical and biological weapons on US bases?

Answer: as above.

Question: How many prosecutions against US forces have been made under UK and US law?

Answer: No numbers are kept

Question: Will the Secretary of State for Defence make public the cost of the sharing agreement between UK and US visiting forces?

Answer: This is confidential under exemption 1 etc (as above)

The extent to which parliamentary questioning can have an important role in uncovering hitherto concealed information about state activities is sharply underlined by a sudden change in state responses to these questions in late 2013. Following the debate and public questioning of the secrecy and lack of accountability of US and UK electronic surveillance, CAAB was informed by a researcher working for a northern MP that the tabling office would no longer accept questions from MP's relating to US issues or to bases in Britain where US personnel are stationed. From where did this order come? Was Parliament informed about this further curtailment of its already limited access to information in this vital area?

However it is also apparent from the records that carefully worded questions over many years fed to MPs such as Norman Baker, the late Lord Kennet, the late Bob

Cryer and those already named, gradually clarified key information about US bases in Britain. A question by David Drew MP asking for clarification of the command structure at named RAF bases elicited the information from Bill Rammell, answering for the Secretary of State for Defence, that 'the sites are commanded by a US officer, usually a US Air Force Officer at colonel rank. An RAF Commander is present at USVF sites, at a lower rank, normally squadron leader. The role of the RAF commander is to liaise with the US base commander and act as head of establishment for MOD employees'. Piece by piece vital information was revealed about their function, the lack of leasing arrangements, the numbers of personnel in each base, the ratio of UK to US staff, categorised by function, the power, or lack of it, of Local Authorities over planning applications for change of amenities or land use on the bases, of who pays for what, who is responsible for security and what power the UK government has over the use of the bases for overseas operations. We know that British MPs and MEPs do not have the right of access to US bases situated in their constituencies, and that much of what happens on the bases is secret and not available for public knowledge. Information has also been gained about the status, financing and command structure of MOD police on the bases, and on the reality of the power of the RAF Liaison Officers. Inadvertently this information casts light on the nature of the 'special relationship' between the UK and the US. These wider issues of sovereignty are of concern to many parliamentarians in both Houses of Parliament. In an article in the Yorkshire Post (20 September 2007) Menzies Campbell noted that in July 2007, just before the Parliamentary recess, 'the Defence

Secretary announced that the government would permit the US to install additional equipment at MHS to support their National Missile Defense programme'. 'There has been no public debate in Britain about the desirability or workability of Missile Defense... our government allows American enclaves on British soil, protected from parliamentary scrutiny or public debate'.

4. *Walking on to the Menwith Hill base*

Another method of gaining information about US bases adopted consistently by the campaigners has been that of walking on to them. This tactic was employed to considerable effect in the Greenham Common campaign. This purposeful activity is both a symbolic protest and a carefully considered act which aims to force the British state, acting through its agents, the MOD and local police, and also the US military to reveal, usually through the courts both what goes on in the bases and, equally importantly, how the state responds to peaceful and legal protest. This is dealt with in the chapters on the court campaigns.

5. *Collaboration*

Contributing to, and learning from, other groups who became concerned about the size and function of US bases in Britain and world-wide is clearly evident in the CAAB records. From the early days questions were asked about US bases not only by peace groups by also by citizens concerned with civil liberties, by parliamentarians concerned with the concealment from parliament of the bases' activities, and by business and commercial groups asking what use was made of intercepted information and whether it was used for other than military purposes.. These questions were generated from the local level, from national groups such as Liberty, journalists' unions and parliamentary groups and at the European level where the most serious challenge to the secret operations of the NSA originated. Between 1999 and 2001 The European Parliament Scientific and Technological Options Office commissioned a series of reports from the British journalist, Duncan Campbell, to look into the concerns of the European parliament that bases such as Menwith Hill were being used by the US to gain information that was not primarily for intelligence purposes, but for gathering commercial information on the US's European competitors. The report identified the name given to the system operated by NASA for intercepting information from commercial satellites: ECHELON. Evidence of commercial espionage was supported by a whistle-blower from Menwith Hill who reported that commercially sensitive information was regularly passed to US corporations. The main report said that electronic surveillance by US intelligence breached the European Convention of Human Rights, and that in particular the English and German parliaments had failed to prevent the improper use of surveillance on their territory. Examination of the CAAB files and records shows the regular correspondence and information sharing between CAAB and these concerned groups, on occasions providing written reports to bodies such as parliamentary select committees.

Professor Paul Rogers said of this campaign in 2001, that it 'represented extremely effective alternative tactics... gathering detailed information and using it to challenge the military and the Government is more important than any protest'.

Menwith Hill and parliamentary oversight

CAAB learned (Source: Newsletter Issue 2, 1997) from information originally kept secret but finally disclosed in court in 1997, that the terms under which the US actually holds the land at MHS rests solely on an exchange of correspondence in 1957 between the then Air Ministry and the US 3rd Airforce, known as 'The Ambassadors' Agreement'.

This was sanctioned by the then Defence Committee, but was not open to either public debate or parliamentary scrutiny. This agreement was due for renewal in 1997, but again there was no open discussion on the grounds that this was confidential and related to arrangements for the mutual defence of the US and Britain. When the renewal date arrived neither the US nor Britain admitted to finding a copy of the original agreement, and security of tenure was granted for another 21 years. This pretence has now been abandoned and the US given an unlimited time frame for occupation. The official secrecy surrounding the legal status of US bases in Britain is in marked contrast to the policies of other European countries such as Germany and Denmark who have debated in parliament and publicly renegotiated the terms and conditions under which US bases remain in their countries.

In 1998 the European Parliament's Civil Liberties Committee expressed concern, especially from the Danish, Dutch and French MEPs about the risk of the abuse of economic information. In Britain, agencies concerned with civil liberties asked whether the technology could be used by the security services to monitor the activities of those whom it suspected of 'internal subversion' especially after

9/11. Richard Norton-Taylor[49] argued that the information gathered by such policies, and shared with security and police agencies, would mean that 'the freedom of the individual would be gravely at risk. The dossier of private information is the badge of the totalitarian state, especially since it is not properly accountable and therefore potentially unlawful'. As examples of the reluctance of governments to reveal what is going on at Menwith Hill, reference is made to a 'Guardian' article[50] which quoted a short answer to a parliamentary question by Nick Harvey (Defence Minister). He briefly stated that the SBIRS facilities at MHS are 'ready for operation... likely by the end of 2011'. This system, which has taken nearly 20 years to build, is the successor of the 'Star Wars' project and is part of a defence shield to direct missiles in space and shoot them down with lasers. Whether or not CAAB is correct in its view that 'the system is far from operational' and 'a fantasy' (quoted in the above article), it is still clear that this information was revealed only incidentally in parliament, and with little attention given to the argument that it heightens the possibility of a pre-emptive strike to disable the system. The RAF space systems director, quoted in the same article, acknowledged that the system may also be more than missile warning and could be used to gather technical intelligence for use by spy agencies.

Another example of the official secrecy surrounding the functions of US bases in Britain is revealed in another 'Guardian' article[51]. CAAB had a significant role in this issue. The campaign contacted Baroness Northover, the coalition spokesperson on International Development, about the presence of cluster bombs on US bases in Britain. They then framed parliamentary questions on this issue. On

December 16 2010, Hansard records that during a debate in the House of Lords questions were asked about the presence of cluster bombs on US bases at Welford and Lakenheath. The House was given the assurance that these had been removed following Britain's signing of the Convention on Cluster Munitions, thus banning their use by this country. The 'Guardian' article shows that 'Wikileaks' revealed US embassy cables showing how defence officials concealed from Parliament the fact that the US is allowed to bring cluster bombs on to UK soil in defiance of this treaty. There were no suggestions that British parliamentarians had lied to the House of Lords, rather that they were given false information.

It is necessary at this stage to attempt to find some explanation for the evasiveness and secrecy shown by the political establishment when the issue of US bases is raised. This examination would also go some way to explaining why the campaigners encountered such determined and sometimes physically violent and unlawful responses to their efforts to bring into the public domain the reality of the functions and status of US bases in Britain. For an introduction to this political issue the analyses of some contemporary political commentators have been used.

Sampson[52] argued that the Iraq war illuminated Britain's relationship with the US in the same way that it revealed the working of its democratic institutions. He considered that Blair's decision to commit Britain to American policy over the war, and to avoid criticism of the policy even if damaging to British interests, was simply the climax to a long-running story going back 40 years. 'Most British politicians were naturally more drawn to America, with their traditional ties, family connections and common language. Prime ministers were always especially inclined to see the world through the eyes of Washington as they inherited the reassuring legacy of the special relationship and shared the sophisticated intelligence and sense of security of the world's most powerful nation and now the only superpower'. Peter Hennessey[53] referred to the 'brilliant satire' of the popular TV series of the 1980's, 'Yes, Prime Minister', and recalled the unquestioning hilarity with which all members of the political establishment greeted the fictional PM's decision to cut Trident, with all the impact of such a decision on US interests. These writers are broadly in agreement in describing Britain post World War 2, as a post colonial power facing economic and political decline, which negotiated, from a position of weakness, a 'special' political relationship with the US. This allowed it, through partial access to US intelligence material, to assume a 'place at the top table' in world political and economic organisations. The financial, political and democratic costs of this alliance are the focus of CAAB's work over the last twenty years.

This does not explain why Britain's relationship with the US in the late twentieth and early twenty-first centuries differs substantially from that of its European neighbours, nor the general public acceptance of the idea of the special relationship and of continued bases in the UK, in contrast to other countries who have renegotiated their status and even their departure. It is instructive to compare how the US responds when its strategic military interests are threatened. In Japan, in March 2010, 90,000 people rallied to demand the cancellation of the proposed relocation of the US marine base at Futenma to a larger base at Henoko.

The newly elected government had pledged to reduce the burden of contributions to the costs of US forces in Okinawa, but under pressure from the Obama administration capitulated on the issue. An unrelated but also revealing document was revealed in an article by Duncan Campbell and Patrick Forbes[54] which detailed an agreement reached between the US and Britain in 1983, setting out what would happen in the event of a nuclear war in Europe. In Britain, US military requirements would be given priority, with US forces given the right to enforce martial law, the power to empress civilian labour and to empty NHS hospitals of their patients to prepare for US military casualties. This is an astonishing surrender of basic UK citizens' rights which had never been made public.

CAAB contributed significantly to the exposure and dissemination of information about the function, legality and expansion of US bases in Britain in the last twenty five years. At the same time it tried to raise in public consciousness issues of national independence, of lack of democratic oversight of the activities on the bases, and of the failings of Parliament to act as a check and to challenge executive power. The description of the court campaigns which follows takes these issues to a different level of detail and more clearly demonstrates the personal costs of the campaign.

Chapter 4

The Court Campaigns 1

We are now embarking on what some of the evaluators (see Chapter 7) believe to be the most significant and distinctive part of CAAB's work, namely the court campaigns. The twenty years of campaigning, the records of hundreds of arrests, and the prolonged and significant court cases make for complex and sometimes confusing reading. In the following chapters which cover a selection of these cases the author writes as a non-lawyer for a presumed audience of readers for whom some of the legal issues, court procedures and police powers and procedures are also unfamiliar ground.

The descriptions of the legal campaigns are therefore organised as follows. The aim is to set out the theoretical framework and the relevant laws and statutes to inform and clarify the reading of the accounts of the actual court cases.

1.   'The theoretical foundations' of civil liberties law.

2.   An overview of a selection of laws passed after World War 2 that have particular relevance to civil liberties, with brief comments to explain this relevance.

3.   A selection of cases and a detailed description of their process and outcome.

It will be shown how the issue of civil liberties and the right to protest emerged as a key and continuing issue for CAAB. It will show how the three key arms of the state (legislature, judiciary and executive) worked in relation to the implementation of legislation relating to civil liberties.

1. The theoretical foundations of civil liberties law

Gearty[55] argued that 'few branches of legal knowledge are as perplexing in their scope... or downright confusing in their application as civil liberties'. It has 'popped in and out of case law and political and legal literature for generations... this rich intellectual heritage gives the subject an uncertainty'. In Chapter 3 reference was made to his description of two distinct versions of civil liberties in Britain and they are worth recalling here, since he believes that they continue to form attitudes today, and that their divergence underlies many instinctive reactions to protest that we see revealed in the responses of politicians, judiciary and police that are evident in the cases described here. Gearty suggested that freedom is viewed on one hand as essentially *individual*. This view has its roots in the social and political upheaval of the seventeenth century and receives its clearest exposition in the later writings of Locke and Burke. It sees individuals as having the right to go about their own business without being subjected to any unnecessary interference by governments. Consent to interfere is essentially a power handed to governments by citizens and it can be revoked. A more *communitarian* view of liberty, developed in nineteenth and twentieth century Britain, with its roots in classical European thought and in the eighteenth century enlightenment, sees that there is more to liberty than being left alone, and that we have to develop a theory of the relationship between our autonomous freedoms, which are individual, and the community and the state. From this strand arises the concern for civil liberties, which in Britain derive from Common Law and from new statute law. These include: the right to vote; the right to liberty and Due Process (ie. to lawful arrest and to a fair trial); the right to freedom of expression; the right to freedom of association.

Gearty believed that there is no 'golden age of freedom lurking in our distant past' and that there always been anxieties (fear of anarchy or radical social change), and opposition from those whose interests would be adversely affected or who fear the state will be left vulnerable to attack. However in tracing the background to the legislation of the last forty or so years, he supported the opinions quoted in chapter 2 by Wilson, Judt et al that the 'subversive power of the Counter Terrorism narrative' has seriously threatened civil liberties in Britain.

2. The legislative framework

The sources for this section are the records of CAAB, Wilson (sup. cit.) and Gearty (sup. cit.) The latter author is relied upon for the comments on statute law and its relevance to civil liberties. The statutes are listed in date order with the exception of the European Convention on Human Rights (1950) and the Human Rights Act (1998) which are dealt with separately at the end.

The Public Order Act (1980)

This Act replaced the Public Order Act of 1936, which arose from the concerns about serious public disorder arising from mass unemployment and from protests and demonstrations from both right-wing fascist organisations and from left-wing communist groups. It made three important changes to the earlier act in that it required protestors to give advance notice of processions to the police, it allowed the police to impose conditions not only on processions but also on *stationary* assemblies, and it also widened the criteria under which processions and assemblies could be modified or forbidden. These now included not only serious public disorder but also a reasonable apprehension that an event would seriously damage property, or involve the intimidation of others 'with a view of compelling them not to do an act they have the right to do'. Gearty saw this Act as the start of a process whereby civil libertarian controls on these statutory powers are progressively loosened and the police increasingly deploy these powers.

The Police and Criminal Evidence Act (1984)

This Act has particular relevance for civil liberties. It deals with the police power of arrest, and the dangers of allowing this power to follow as a matter of course whenever a crime is suspected. Gearty judged that one of the most controversial aspects of the 1984 Act was its extension of the police power of arrest to 'non-arrestable' as well as 'arrestable' cases. Included in the former was 'obstruction of the highway'. This clearly has implications for peaceful protest and demonstrations. As a result of a recent amendment to this Act, one of the grounds for arrest for *any* offence now judged sufficient is 'to allow prompt and effective investigation of the suspected offence and the conduct of the person in question'. This power covers a very wide range of behaviour, and with arrest comes the power to search the person and his house, to seize his property and to detain and interrogate for up to four days. Gearty thought that at the time of writing (2007) the implications of this Act were still being absorbed, but that in the worst scenario, these powers could wipe out public protest. It could turn technical breaches of the law into a platform for disproportionate police action. He asked what will happen if the police begin to use these powers in a routine way, eg in cases of peaceful picketing, or in a peaceful demonstration by employees against their employer, and if the prosecuting authorities do not then take a liberal view of the case.

The Criminal Justice and Public Order Act (1994)
Gearty regarded this Act as pivotal in regard to the freedom of public protest. For the first time the police secured the power to end protest meetings. The device used was via new controls on 'trespassory assemblies', meeting on lands where the public had no right of access or only a limited right. This effectively brought public highways into its remit. Under this Act, if a chief police officer believes that an assembly of 20 or more persons may result in disturbance to the life of a community, and is without prior permission from the occupier of the land, and where it may result in damage to the land, a building or a monument, then he may apply to the Local Authority to prohibit such an assembly in a district for up to four days and within a radius of five miles. The Act also, among other provisions, removed the right to silence of

a defendant, when arrested and gave the police the power to declare certain area 'stop and search zones', where they can search vehicles and pedestrians without even suspecting they have committed an offence.

Gearty noted that under successive pieces of legislation, trespass has been transformed into a criminal act, which has serious implications for one of the main techniques of protestors eg. 'sit-ins', collective trespasses, trespassing on a designated site, and engaging in disruptive trespass. The effect of this Act is that those who choose trespass as their way of reaching out to public sentiment need to acknowledge that they may incur a criminal record.

The Crime and Disorder Act (1998)
The Anti Social Behaviour Act (2003)
Gearty treated these Acts together as arising from a concern in the 1990s to design new systems which would deliver convictions more easily, particularly aiming at low-level bad behaviour that had hitherto been ignored by the criminal law.

Under the 1998 Act an Anti-Social Behaviour Order could be obtained by application by the police or the local authority to a magistrate's court, aimed at 'persons acting in an anti social manner... likely to cause harassment, alarm or disturbance to one or more persons not of the same household as himself'. The Order can be as broad as necessary, with swingeing punishments attached to its breach, including (if tried by jury) a sentence of up to five years in jail.

The issues of liberty and the right to protest are clear. They could be used against those who are engaged in political protest, although again Gearty noted that at the time of writing there was no evidence of its widespread use. However the subsequent records of the bye-laws cases refer to the use of an ASBO against Lindis Percy. In a 'Guardian' article of 18/12/2005 the judge was quoted as saying that the threatened use of an ASBO was 'using a club to beat down the expression of legitimate protest'.

The Terrorism Act (2000)

This Act embodies many of the provisions of the Terrorism Act of 1974 which was intended to deal with the terrorist threat posed by the Irish Republican Army. The 2000 Act was followed by further statutory interventions after 9/11 and the terrorist attacks in London in 2005.

The Act covers 'actual or threatened conduct involving either serious violence against the person or serious damage to property', where that aim is 'to influence government or an international organisation or to intimidate the public or a section of the public' and where the purpose is to 'advance a political, religious or ideological cause'. Gearty suggested that the issue here is that action is also to be regarded as terrorist with the same intention of influence or intimidation identified above, if it endangers life, creates a serious risk to the health and safety of the public or is 'designed to disrupt an electronic system'. Violence is no longer an essential feature of the definition. 'With these remarkable expansions of definition, terrorism burst its original banks in the criminal law and overflowed in the direction of direct action, civil disobedience and of political protest generally' (p 47).

'History may judge this piece of legislation to have been as important a benchmark in the decline of civil liberties protection in Britain as its 1974 predecessor' (p46).

Gearty argued that the threat to civil liberties lies not in empowering the law enforcement agencies to deal with violent terrorists, but rather in that terrorism suspects are now dealt with in a way that is entirely different from the manner of treating 'ordinary' criminals. 'It is corrosive of our political and legal culture'. It brings within the definition of terrorism the freedom not only of political activists but of those on the margins of such groups who may find their freedom threatened by an overzealous reading of the law by police, or the security or Crown Prosecution Service. It also has an impact on 'due process' safeguards. Gearty concluded from the cases brought under this law that 'there is plenty of evidence of the courts being very slow to challenge ministerial and police assumptions about what the exigencies of national security now require in this new era of alleged 'global terrorism' (p 48).

The Prevention of Terrorism Act (2005)

The prime object of this Act was to provide for measures to prevent individuals from involvement in terrorist- related activities by imposing restrictions on their activities. This would be effective by means of two types of orders: 'derogating orders ', the more restrictive of the two, such as house arrest, and 'non derogating control orders', such as tagging, restriction on place of residence, of work or of travel. They are made by the Secretary of State, with a court involved only after the order has been made. Gearty argued that this act is a major departure from criminal law in that it provides for the imposition of severe restraints, some in direct contravention of the Human Rights Act (1998), on the basis of suspicion that would not necessarily form the basis of a criminal charge. At the time of writing there was no evidence that this had strayed into the realm of political behaviour, but the possibility is there.

The Serious Organised Crime and Police Act (2005)

This Act also contains provision for intervention in public protest. It is of particular relevance to peace protestors and to CAAB in particular. Section 28 focussed on nuclear power stations and military sites, allowing the Secretary of State to class them as 'designated sites' which would give the police new powers against trespassers on these sites, thus increasing the potential for the criminalisation of peaceful protest. For example, walking peacefully around the perimeter of a site could constitute a criminal activity, and cases have reached the courts where low key protestors declined to give advance notice of their intentions and were prosecuted.

The Act is probably most well- known for its application in the case of Brian Haw, who persistently protested in Parliament Square, and of protestors reading out, in Whitehall, the names of soldiers killed in Iraq.

The use of bail restrictions and of 'bind over' orders

These are included here although they derive not from statute law but from powers derived from Common Law or from local legislation. Gearty noted that these ancient procedures have been used continuously by prosecuting authorities to disrupt protest of which they disapproved. An example has been to use the imposition of bail conditions or the bind over power against protestors holding banners or distributing leaflets at an arms fair. It allows the police to stop a demonstration without proof of criminal conduct.

The European Convention of Human Rights (1950)
The Human Rights Act (1998)

The majority of rights and freedoms later incorporated into the Human Rights Act derive from the 1950 convention. It was in part inspired by the awareness in post-war Europe of the dangers which arise when a particular government, with majority support, wants to impose particular values, that constitute a threat to minorities. The answer to this 'majoritarian problem' was seen to be that of Human Rights. In 1998 the majority of rights and freedoms set out in the European Convention were incorporated into UK law. Gearty argued that the primary thrust of this legislation has been to promote and defend civil liberties.

The rights set out in this act include: The right to liberty (Article 5); The right to privacy (Article 8); The right to freedom of religion (Article 9); The right of expression (Article 10); The right of association (Article 11); The right of assembly (Article 11)

It also embraces the right of any minority not to be discriminated against in the enjoyment of these rights. The Act requires judges to interpret the legislation's compatibility with the Human Rights Act, and to make a 'declaration of incompatibility' if they judge this to be so. This does not have legal consequences but it creates a climate of opinion of what is acceptable. The result of the introduction of the Human Rights Act has been 'a boon in human rights law as the courts have become familiar with human rights arguments across a whole range of litigation areas' (p 24).

As a general comment on this raft of legislation, Gearty made two general points that lead us beyond a solely legal approach, and which are important to bear in mind, albeit critically, when reading the accounts of CAAB's court campaigns.

First, that 'there are layers of official good sense, moderation and sensitivity to civil liberties that make the gap between law and the practice on the ground pleasingly wider than some civil libertarians will allow' (p 148).

And secondly, that 'the level of protection for freedom of political speech is only partly dependent on the law. There are important roles for executive and judicial functionaries to moderate the disproportionate impact of notionally illiberal laws' (ibid). Of crucial importance in the sustaining of freedom is the cultural assumption that civil liberties such as freedom of speech and of assembly are essentials in our community life.

When reading the following account of the court campaigns it is also important to consider the issue of national sovereignty, which is at the heart of two of these cases. It has been maintained from the earliest years of the protests against Menwith Hill that the status and presence of the bases essentially undermines the status of Britain as a sovereign nation. For a definition of this term use is made of the 'New Fontana Dictionary of Modern Thought' (1999) which states;

'Sovereignty: literally the possession of ultimate legal authority; a state is sovereign when its rulers owe allegiance to no superior power and are themselves supreme within the local legal order'.

The UN charter states that a super power should station its overseas bases within the terms of a formal treaty. We can contrast this definition with the content of a speech made in the House of Commons in 1993 by Bob Cryer, then MP for Bradford South. In a long speech he referred to the campaigning of Lindis Percy and Anne Lee asking, 'What does it say for parliamentary democracy when people have no rights against these arrogant organisations' (he is referring here to large US firms using information based on the communications monitoring at Menwith Hill), 'which are given authority by a clique of people called the Government who have not come to Parliament for any authority?' The then Minister of State for the Armed Forces dismissed this as 'ill-informed, second- hand fantasy' but the key issue of the nature of the terms on which the bases are held, the openness to parliamentary oversight and the reality of the supremacy of English law are explored carefully through the legal cases which are now described.

A selection of court cases from the CAAB records is now examined in detail.

Case Study 1: The military land bye-laws cases

It is difficult to do justice to this case study, in part due to its length and the number of legal cases involved, but also to the way in which what was originally an issue about the legality of bye-laws on military land gradually widened to encompass broader legal issues. These include the right to peaceful protest, the right to assembly and the general issue of how the competing interests of public order and the right to protest are to be reconciled. During the progress of the cases we begin to see clarified some of the issues outlined

69

in the legal introduction, in particular the way in which existing laws that touch on issues of civil liberties operate in practice and how official functionaries interpret the law.

The bye-laws campaign has its roots in the Greenham Common protests of the 1980s, and was pursued by CAAB in a saga of arrests and court cases that continue to the present day.

The military land bye-laws, enacted in the 1980s under powers defined by the Military Land Act of 1892, were introduced by the Secretary of State for Defence to give legal protection to military bases by making trespass on them a criminal offence. These bye-laws were used effectively in the 1980s to deter protest, particularly against the introduction of cruise missiles at Greenham Common. Menwith Hill was ringed with the first set of bye-laws in 1986, again to deter developing protest at the base. A significant campaigner during the 1980s, John Bugg, an ex-policeman, argued that these military bye-laws had failed to follow correct procedures and were therefore invalid. Using this argument, three women at Greenham successfully tested the bye-laws in 1987 by walking onto the base. This resulted in arrests and a total of 900 cases which were accumulated and brought to trial. This key trial ended, on appeal, in the House of Lords. The bye-laws were declared invalid, costs were awarded to the women and previous convictions under the military bye-laws were overturned.

In 1990, Lindis Percy was first arrested for walking onto the base at Menwith Hill and, having built up a file of 111 charges, appeared before the local magistrate's court. The Director for Public Prosecutions (DPP) had to concede the charges on a legal technicality but then appealed the case to the High Court. The judgement in 1993 was that the bye-laws were declared 'defective on their face' and therefore no longer safe as the basis for prosecution. Two years later, in 1995, the second set of bye-laws was imposed on Menwith Hill. In 1997 two campaigners from the Menwith Hill Peace Camp, Helen John and Anne Lee, brought a test case against these bye-laws, again with 26 pending prosecutions for the same offence. The case was heard before Judge Crabtree at a five-day hearing at York Crown Court, with evidence heard from Tony Benn MP and Duncan Campbell, the investigative journalist referred to in Chapter 3. The arguments against the bye-laws were accepted but this time on the technical point that 70% of the base was 'under sheep' and therefore the military bye-laws were invalid. This judgement was later overturned on appeal.

In 1991 the then Secretary of State for Defence, Tom King, brought a civil action against Lindis Percy following several instances of arrest after she had walked on the base at Menwith Hill. He applied for an injunction to prevent her from doing so. The case was heard in 1993 at York County Court before Judge Crabtree. This time the judge acknowledged the seriousness of the arguments advanced by the campaigner concerning the legality and accountability of the arrangements by which the base was occupied by the Americans. He referred the case to the High Court commenting that 'If Ms Percy is right in her defence, it will mean that all the arrangements between the UK and the US will have to re-negotiated'. The campaigner was forced to concede the case in 1998 when the then Secretary of State for Defence, Malcolm Rifkind, successfully applied for a 'Public Interest Immunity Certificate'. This injunction and four other permanent injunctions against Lindis Percy, originally intended to be temporary and followed by trial, still stand.

An observer would anticipate that from thenceforth it would be a relatively simple matter for the MOD police to deal with any further attempts to walk on the base by arresting them under the now-valid Military Land Bye-laws. Instead, no further prosecutions were made using them. It seems a reasonable assumption that the authorities were unsure of their success in any future challenge to their validity. Instead, the CAAB records now show a long campaign, lasting to the present day, during which the campaigner consistently tested in court the grounds on which the authorities tried to limit or to make illegal their right to make a peaceful entry on to the base that would enable them to research, clarify and make public its changing functions and the legal accountability of base personnel.

Lindis Percy, in a paper delivered at the Peace Studies Department at Bradford University in 1996, acknowledged that this area of the campaign was becoming more and more complicated. 'The starting point was opposing nuclear weapons, but this led to taking on the military and legal systems and the government'. The records show that in the 17 years of the campaign up to 2012, the campaigners engaged in behaviour that may seem trivial or provocative, for example, removing a bye-law sign to continually test the validity of the law; openly walking on the base to provoke arrest and a subsequent court appearance; stopping cars entering or leaving the base for a clearly limited time in order to display an upside-down US flag, indicating opposition, or to engage the driver in conversation; openly walking over a yellow line drawn around the base to test the limits of the injunction. The records show that in most of these instances, Lindis Percy and, to a lesser extent, Anni Rainbow were targetted for arrest when other protestors acting in a similar way were ignored. A CAAB report of 2003 shows the continued determination of the campaigners to bring the bye-laws issue to court. After 1995 Lindis Percy was arrested over 150 times at Menwith Hill but no case proceeded to trial. In one case, she walked on the base at Fylingdales and stated clearly to the MOD officer who approached her that she was committing an offence under the bye-laws. The officer said that there were new guidelines not to use these laws but rather section 68 of the Criminal Justice and Public Order Act of 1994. At Scarborough Police Station she was told that the 'new guidelines' had been introduced a week before by the Chief Constable of the MOD police.

To attempt to present this long campaign in a comprehensible form the analysis will set out as follows: the different grounds for arrest used by the authorities after the abandonment of the bye-laws as a ground for prosecution; the actions taken by the protestors in response to these arrests and prosecutions, and, importantly the issues they raise both for peaceful protestors and for citizens concerned for civil liberties. The legal framework set out earlier in this chapter will be used.

Throughout, it is apparent that the aim of the campaigner was to test, by non-violent action which stays within the law, the legality not only of the arrests but also of the subsequent actions of the judiciary and of the executive arm of the state. Light is shed on legal and court processes and the reality of citizens gaining access to the law. This will go some way towards confirming or refuting the discussion begun earlier in the chapter about the extent to which recent legislation is in reality eroding the civil rights of peaceful protestors. The arrests sometimes arose from individual actions of the protestor, and sometimes from the weekly demonstrations outside Menwith Hill when more individuals were involved, or from larger demonstrations organised to protest against an action such as the invasion of Iraq, or on the annual July 4 'Independence from America' demonstration. In general, protestors at these events were not involved in activities that aimed at provoking arrest.

Reference has already been made to the interlocutory (temporary) injunction imposed on Lindis Percy by the High Court in 1993. This prevented her from entering US bases, called RAF bases at Menwith Hill, Alconbury, Feltwell, Mildenhall and Lakenheath. The activities of CAAB at bases other than Menwith Hill are not included in this book but are reported in the campaign records. A limit of 15 metres was placed around the base at Menwith Hill, which she was not allowed to cross. It is not difficult to anticipate the possible confusion and the potential for legal challenge which could, and did, arise from this restriction. Did it apply to attendance at the weekly demonstration at Menwith Hill? If not, was Lindis Percy's right to peaceful assembly being ignored? What of Lindis Percy's right to freedom of religion if she was forbidden to attend the regular Quaker Meetings for Worship there? Would a defined line beyond which she might not go prove to be problematic, eg if it included a public highway?

A series of arrests in 2004 show how the MOD and local police reacted in a concerted attempt to prevent Lindis from taking part in the weekly demonstrations, some of which were attended by only a handful of demonstrators. The first arrest was for *'obstructing a police officer in the course of his duty'* while standing in front of cars leaving the base waving the US flag, upside down, with polite political statements written on it. At Harrogate police station this was changed to *'obstructing the public highway'* and *bail* was imposed with the condition that she did not go within 15 metres of the base. This pattern of arrest continued for several weeks, and the campaigners' experience was that the CPS often applied for remand in custody for alleged trespass or other minor offences. On one occasion the police imposed more restrictive bail conditions. Lindis Percy rested her defence on the key case 'Hirst and Agu vs the Chief Constable of West Yorks 1986'. This had stated clearly the right of protestors to use public highways provided there were limits to their actions so that the right to peaceful protest could be balanced against the right of citizens to go about their daily lives. The campaigner was careful to keep to these limits (particularly the 'de minimus' provision of stopping cars for only a limited amount of time). She also challenged the imposition of stricter bail conditions.

This challenge was accepted at Harrogate Magistrates' court, which reinstated the previous conditions stating that 'the new ones were disproportionate to the offence'.

By January 2005 arrests had been made on eight consecutive weeks. After the final arrest Lindis Percy was detained in Harrogate Police Station overnight and on the following day, the CPS applied to the Magistrates' Court for bail conditions that forbade the campaigner from going within 50 metres of the base. Again, this was refused by the magistrates. The cases accruing from these arrests were 'stacked' to be heard at a four-day hearing at Harrogate Magistrates' Court before Judge Anderson in April 2005. The judge found Lindis Percy guilty of only five offences, one of 'obstruction of the Highway and four of 'obstruction of a police officer'. Unexpectedly the CPS then applied for an *Anti-Social Behaviour Order (ASBO)* against Lindis Percy, with a large areas of prohibition around Menwith Hill (a ten mile radius for ten years). Following a day's adjournment for probation reports, and with considerable media interest in the case, the judge refused the application with the comment already noted that 'the courts should not be used to beat down the expression of legitimate comment and the dissemination of views on matters of public concern'. Nevertheless the Judge ordered that Lindis Percy be *tagged and subject to curfew* for eight weeks. This was immediately appealed to York Crown Court and the hearing set for November 2005. At this hearing the defence solicitor argued for the need to balance the right to protest and the rights of people to go about their lawful business. It was agreed that tagging and the imposition were disproportionate, as 'she has the right to protest'. Only one of Lindis Percy's appeals against the charges for which she had been convicted at Harrogate Magistrates' Court was allowed. It was ruled that she did not have the right to stop cars and that the police have the duty to keep traffic moving. However her costs were reduced from £3,500 to £800.

These are mixed results for the campaign. Important principles were stated in court of the right to peaceful protest, against the use of ASBOs, tagging and curfews, and a refusal to endorse the severe bail conditions imposed by the MDPA and local police and requested by the CPS.

It is also important to note that after these judgements, arrests continued for *Obstruction of the Highway*. At a three-day-hearing at Harrogate Magistrates' court in September 2006, before Judge Manning, the police admitted difficulties over agreeing on a definition of the 'yellow line' (the limit defined in the injunction). Video evidence was used and eight MDPA officers were called to support the CPS case. Again in 2011, when tried for the same offence she was found guilty and fined £855. This time officers from the Counter Terrorism Unit were called to give evidence, and again video evidence was used and disputed. Finally, in a case which ended in 2012, Lindis Percy was again charged at the weekly demonstration on the ground of *obstructing three MDPA officers in the course of their duty.* This case involved issues that had also become apparent in cases in which CAAB had been involved outside Menwith Hill. These were about the lack of availability of documents made by the CPS for the defence (in this case documents concerning the extended powers and jurisdiction of the MDPA), the lack of crucial video evidence related to 'the offence', and the conduct of the CPS in ignoring the District Judge's directions. The case was heard by Judge Jane Goodwin, and Lindis Percy conducted her own defence. Judge Goodwin ruled that there was no case to answer. Her reasoning was that the prosecution's case was 'weak, vague and contained inconsistencies' and that there were serious failings in the evidence provided by the MDPA. All charges were dismissed and costs awarded to Lindis Percy.

Lindis Percy then complained to the Chief of the MOD Police about the conduct of a named Constable of the Divisional Support Group, engaged in policing the protest at Menwith Hill, together with MOD officers. In particular she complained about the circumstances of her arrest and about the MOD police case preparation and conduct during her trial at Harrogate Magistrate's Court in April 2012. This complaint was referred to the Professional Standard Department of the Ministry of Defence Police. Their response to this complaint acknowledges behaviour 'unprofessional and embarrassing for the Force' and agrees that the case 'highlighted very significant weaknesses in officer training which no doubt extends well beyond Menwith Hill'. Reference was also made to a separate report within the MOD which made 'eleven very pertinent recommendations that should be seriously considered if the Force is to avoid a similar set of circumstances'.

Lindis also formally complained to the Crown Prosecution Service about the grounds for prosecution in this case, especially the use CCTV evidence and the way this was presented to her for use at the trial. This complaint was referred to the Case Management Panel of the CPS, and two separate responses were sent to Lindis Percy in August 2013 from the Deputy Chief Prosecutor (Yorkshire and Humberside CPS), and from the head of the Welfare, Rural and Health Division of the CPS. The responses expressed unequivocal apologies for the way in which the CPS had handled the case. In particular they acknowledge that 'the case was handled poorly and Lindis Percy's Right to a Fair Trial was not protected'. They agree that the disclosure of the CCTV footage was inadequate and that there were significant failures in complying with the judge's orders. It was agreed that there were 'issues with the MOD police and a need for greater training for officers in respect of their powers of arrest and shortcomings in the preparation and handling of the case'. In conclusion, 'sincere apologies' were offered and it was promised that the 'significant failings' would be 'drawn to the attention of the Chief Crown Prosecutor for Yorkshire so that he can put in place effective arrangements for a full post case review'.

This case and the subsequent correspondence make dramatic reading. They confirm what had already been apparent from previous cases; the failures in training and supervision of MOD police officers, and weaknesses in CPS internal decision making and professional procedures. We do not yet know how or even if, recommended changes will be implemented but this case is a clear example of the effectiveness of informed and tenacious opposition to unlawful and unprofessional responses to peaceful protest.

These cases are reported in detail and they help us to start the process of answering some of the questions posed by Gearty and set out earlier in this chapter. We can see the extent to which legislation passed with terrorism in mind is invoked to control peaceful protest. We can see the difficulties citizens can face in their right to 'due process', and in the financial costs involved. Importantly, we can see how the executive arm of the state, and the judiciary, vary in their reaction to the legal and operational challenges posed by peaceful protest. However we have to place this particular strand of the CAAB campaign in a wider context. How far are the experiences outlined above supported by the experience of other groups engaged in peaceful protest?

The Report by the House of Lords and House of Commons Select Committee on Human Rights. Demonstrating respect for rights? A human rights approach to policing protest. (2009).

This committee's report contains valuable evidence and comment which enables us to go some way in answering these questions. The committee called for submissions, written and verbal from a wide range of organisations, 56 in all, such as 'Liberty', 'Justice', 'Justice not Vengeance', The National Union of Journalists, Medact (a global health charity tackling issues at the centre of international debates), CND and CAAB (Lindis Percy also gave verbal evidence) and, for balance, representatives from the Association of Chief Police Officers (ACPO), the Police Federation, the then Minister for Policing Crime and Security, and an organisation which has been on the receiving end of protest, Huntingdon Life Sciences. There were no contributions from the Ministry of Defence Police.

The verbal evidence from 'Liberty' and 'Justice' show a clear response that, in their opinion, although the Human Rights Act has given protestors the constitutional right to freedom of assembly, nevertheless the sweeping public order powers given to the police have counterbalanced this. Dr. Metcalfe, from 'Justice', thought that their much larger range of statutory powers now interfered with peaceful protest and that security concerns since 9/11 have tended to override the right of freedom of assembly. In particular he focussed on the use of *Section 44 of the CJPO Act of 1994* and the use of 'stop and search' powers at large protest gatherings. James Welch, senior lawyer at 'Liberty' echoed concerns about the 'chilling effects' of Section 44 on protestors. *The Serious Crime and Public Order Act (2005)* received much detailed attention, both in the implementation of specific sections such as the *'designated areas'* provision and in the more general principle of the introduction of criminal sanctions when arrangements for protest were not correctly followed. It was felt that this led to challenges that not only mocked the law but also undermined the principle of consensus between protestors and society as embodied by the police, on which peaceful protest depended. The National Union of Journalists' representative was concerned at the treatment of accredited journalists by the police during demonstrations, particularly the use of 'stop and search' powers, being photographed, being blocked from photographing, and generally the creation of an 'intimidatory atmosphere'. This drew an unusually sharp response from Lord Lester that such behaviour by the police, if proven was a 'blatant disregard of the Human Rights Act and gross interference with the freedom of speech'.

The reports of the long interviews with representatives from the police are useful in providing insights into their ethos, and their evident concern to stress the importance placed on police awareness of Human Rights issues both in basic training and in ongoing legal and operational advice during protests. They also commented on the importance given to early communication with protestors about planned protest. There was an awareness of the lack of clarity between different local forces, and within units when faced with changing and often chaotic situations, where the distinction between peaceful protest and (to them) potential or threatened violence was not clear.

Two pieces of written evidence are of immediate relevance to CAAB. Angie Zelter (see Chapter 5) from the Faslane campaign set out, in a memo, clear statements about the importance of peaceful protest, arguing that it brings to the attention of the public and government issues to which they are not seen to be responding sufficiently, and provides a social feedback mechanism that can do much to relieve social tensions. In particular she argued that protests at sites such as Parliament, corporate HQ and military bases are important because it is there 'that many abuses of power can take place'. She gave examples of good co-operative policing from the Strathclyde police but her general criticisms were directed at the use of counter-terrorism powers to police protests, at the lack of an independent process to handle complaints against the police and the failure of the internal complaints system.

Yorkshire CND also submitted evidence of their experience of protesting at Fylingdales and at Menwith Hill, aimed at raising public awareness of the US missile defence programme and the importance of the Yorkshire bases in this. Their experience was that the introduction of SOCPA made a marked difference in policing at the bases, with more astringent responses to such actions as walking around the perimeter of the bases. They noted that 'stop and search' powers were used against protestors and that large barriers were used to 'pen' protestors, along with intrusive photographing by both the MDPA and the North Yorkshire police. They gave as a further illustration the arrest in 2006, using *SOCPA section 28* of two campaigners, Helen John and Sylvia Boyes, who walked on to the base of Menwith Hill with placards. CND argued that their conviction criminalised trespass at designated sites across Britain. They noted that in this case the judge imposed the minimum sentence of a conditional discharge for three months and a £50 fine. This they saw as an enormous waste of resources. It also gives an example of what Gearty called the ameliorating power of the judiciary in cases of illiberal law. Finally they gave an example of highly visible police levels at a planned demonstration in 2008. The ration was 3:1 in relation to protestors, with the use of horses, cameras and videos, creating what they felt to be an intimidatory atmosphere to deter protest. This level of policing had been usual at the July 4th Demonstrations at Menwith Hill for many years previously.

Before proceeding to the Committee's conclusion, it salutary to hear the contribution from Huntingdon Life Services, one of the few organisations who had been on the receiving end of protests. Their spokesman argued that the rights of protestors were taken more care of than were those protested against, and there were forthright views of protestors as 'Leveller fantasists', engaging in 'theatrics to gain publicity', with 'everybody feeling good and nothing achieved... all at a cost of hundreds of millions of pounds of public money'.

The Committee's conclusions

The Committee devoted considerable space to an overview of the array of legislation which they noted, although not designed to deal with protest, had nevertheless 'become part of the police officer's toolkit'. These have already been summarised earlier in this chapter, but the report also draws attention to the use of *civil injunctions* issued under the

Protection from Harassment Act (1997) which has been used as a means of stopping protest without the protestors having the right to put their case in court. They also questioned the use of section 28 of SOCPA and its use as a blanket ban on protest in designated areas, questioning whether walking around the perimeter fence at Menwith Hill could be seen as criminal activity, and pointing out that an individual carrying a potentially dangerous instrument could be arrested under other laws.

In terms of general principles the Committee argued that in the difficult balance between the rights of protestors and the rights of citizens going about their lawful business, under Human Rights law the balance should always be in favour of those seeking the right to protest. 'Inconvenience and disruption alone are not sufficient grounds to prevent a protest'. The committee noted the 'significant mismatch' between the perceptions of protestors and the police over the way that protest is managed, and that the police not only did not always get the balance right between the protestors and those protested against, but that they also always failed to identify the fundamental liberties at stake. But they also acknowledged the role played by overbroad or vague legislation leading to wide discretion given to police officers, with an unclear line between lawful and unlawful conduct. They remarked on progressively and increasingly severe legislation resulting in a bewildering array of overlapping powers and offences which made the police task harder.

The Committee urged research on the real extent of police knowledge and awareness of human rights as thrown up by protest, and argued for a mechanism for independent scrutiny of police conduct. They also emphasised the importance of dialogue between police and protestors before the event. In general their conclusion was that, while there was no evidence of Human Rights abuses by the police, there was nevertheless a failure on their part to facilitate and protect peaceful protest, thus jeopardising protestors' right to freedom of assembly, and in particular they were concerned at the lack of understanding by the police of the way in which the use of riot gear at protests would affect perceptions of their intentions and thus the way protestors behaved.

This account of the Committee's findings is included so that CAAB's long and costly campaign to challenge the legality and appropriateness of the official response to peaceful protest and challenge within the law, can be broadly confirmed and placed within the wider context of serious and important debates about the state of civil liberties in Britain at the turn of the twenty-first century.

Chapter 5

The Court Campaigns 2

Case Study 2: The 'Immunity of Visiting Forces' campaign

The second legal campaign by CAAB that will be explored concerns the legal challenges to the powers of visiting foreign forces in the UK and also the function, accountability and status of Ministry Defence Police on US bases. From early days in the campaign fundamental questions have been asked that are plainly of wider public concern. Who is responsible for security on the bases? What role do British police have? Do MOD police behave any differently from their 'mainstream' colleagues? Who pays for them? Do US security officers have any power outside the bases? What are the lines of responsibility and accountability in the bases? And, following the main structure of argument in this book, what methods did CAAB use to clarify these issues, and with what results? The events of the last decade with revelations in Afghanistan and Iraq of the way that foreign soldiers and security forces from any nations are capable of conducting themselves in relation to indigenous citizens remind us of the necessity for clear guidelines and sanctions governing conduct and for transparent processes of accountability and redress.

Before examining how the status and powers of US military personnel on their bases here are defined it is revealing to describe a face to face incident. In 1995 the two campaigners were walking on a public road near the US base at Mildenhall in Suffolk. They were immediately followed by a US soldier on a bicycle, in army uniform, in a reflector jacket marked 'Police' and carrying a gun. The campaigners asked him to stop following them and, when he failed to do so, made a Citizen's Arrest for breach of the peace. They then waited for the arrival of the civil police. With the arrival of more US security police, the incident escalated. Lindis Percy was thrown to the ground, handcuffed and finally dragged inside the base. Anni Rainbow, in a wheel-chair, attempted to come to her aid and tipped over. All this was videoed by US security. When the civil police arrived they at first did not intervene, but finally arrested Lindis for the theft of the bicycle, and later charged her with assaulting two police officers and an MOD officer. In all, the charges were changed five times before the case came to court. When it finally did so in June 1996, all the charges against Lindis Percy were dismissed and the Stipendiary Magistrate commented that 'the level, duress and duration of the violence to Ms Percy was shocking'.

What happened to the US personnel? As no charges were brought, Lindis Percy took out a private prosecution, but when it came to court, the solicitor acting for the US personnel entered a Certificate of Immunity, which was accepted. This was appealed to the High Court but was lost.

The case raises some serious questions. What were US police doing on a British highway with guns? Why were they not charged or disciplined for violence against a British citizen? What were the responsibilities of the British police in this situation? What is the extent of the immunity from prosecution of US forces?

A second incident which reached a conclusion in the summer of 2010 was equally significant. In June 2006 Lindis Percy entered RAF Croughton, near Northampton, as a peaceful protestor. When stopped, she identified herself and agreed to leave the base. She was then thrown to the ground by US security police, searched and handcuffed. (Later, during her detention at Banbury Police station, a police surgeon examined her and confirmed that she suffered from facial palsy as a result of pressure to her neck.) Two MDPA personnel were present and one tried to have the handcuffs removed, but was overruled by the US police. Asked to leave the base, Lindis immediately returned to the base to ensure that the case came to court. She was then arrested under section 8 of *SOCPA* and charged with aggravated trespass.

The case came to court and collapsed on a technicality, but the police refused to pursue the charge of assault. A private prosecution was initiated by Lindis Percy against US police involved in the incident but Corby Magistrates refused to issue the summons, giving no reasons for their lack of action. The campaigner then applied for a judicial review in the High Court. The judge was highly critical of Corby Magistrates and ordered them to issue the summons, awarding costs to Lindis Percy. The case then came to Northampton magistrates' court in 2008 but none of the defendants appeared in court, although ordered to do so.

The CPS applied to take over the case from the campaigner on the grounds that it was a contentious private case with political implications. At the subsequent four hearings none of the US officers accused appeared in court although ordered to do so, and finally the CPS entered a certificate of immunity, and the case was dropped.

Once again there are serious questions about the accountability of US forces, the apparent lack of legal remedy for British citizens and the seemingly all conquering power of the Visiting Forces Act (VFA). This Act, passed in 1952 along with the Status of Forces Agreement (SOFA, 1951) loosely defined the status of the US air force in Britain, with arrangements further defined by the Memorandum of Understanding. One can only guess at the nature of information available to the magistrates, and one has to ask what influences operated that informed the actions of the magistrates and the officers of the CPS. The case did not end there. In February 2009 Lindis Percy took out a civil claim in the small claims court against the US airman who inflicted the injury and in 2010 he offered to settle out of court with costs to the campaigner. This was accepted and the £700 donated to CAAB. As well as the issues of accountability and legality which were raised by both these cases, they also illustrate the financial and emotional costs of a long and determined court campaign, and the degree of legal and procedural sophistication that campaigners need to acquire to mount legal challenges.

The issue is further clarified by a case involving both campaigners who walked on to the base at RAF Feltwell in 1994. The interest in this case lies not primarily in the legal issues raised but in an analysis of the innumerable letters written by Anni Rainbow in the two years following the incident. At Feltwell both campaigners were handled roughly by the US security forces (Lindis Percy was blindfolded and handcuffed and Anni, in a wheelchair was pushed aside), even though the Ministry of Defence police were present. One of these police officers did respond to a plea from Lindis Percy to intervene. The MOD police told the US security officers that they were behaving illegally and that the campaigners had agreed to leave the base after protesting peacefully. Lindis then attempted to pursue a legal complaint against the US officers. Her attempts to do so, and the responses from the MOD, from the RAF liaison officer, from the Minister for the Armed Forces, and finally from the USAF, make absorbing reading, not only for the patient, rigorous and determined questioning but also for the endless prevarication and obstruction which she encountered. Anni attempted to raise, and gain answers to, some key questions that the incident had raised. Do the MOD police have a duty to escort peaceful protestors from US bases? Do they have the power to stop US personnel from acting unlawfully? Is it lawful for a US security guard to handcuff a peaceful protestor? Is peaceful, non-violent protest to be defined as criminal activity? Were the MOD police party to the US videoing non-violent protest? What happened to these videos?

One response from the MOD was surprising. In response to a question about the legal powers of the MOD Lindis was advised, in rather dismissive language, to consult her own solicitor for information. Another, from the Minister of Defence suggested that 'Ms Rainbow should stop manufacturing confrontational situations'. Parallel activity by Juliet McBride, a campaigner in Southampton, clarified where the sources of the powers of US forces in Britain are located (in SOFA and VFA described above). It took three years for Anni Rainbow to obtain a copy of the US Third Air Force Instruction entitled 'Complaints by British Nationals against USAF personnel 'and her requests to pursue her complaint formally were ignored. Finally, the RAF Commander agreed that her complaint would be passed to the Complaints Review Board. Again, no further contact resulted and her attempts to prepare her case by gaining access to all relevant papers and video evidence, using the USA Freedom of Information Act, were blocked. There is interesting complementary evidence from Juliet McBride who had similar experiences at Lakenheath in 1994, resulting in her asking similar questions about the secretive nature of the Complaints Review Board, which she argued effectively breached section 11 of the VFA.

An article by Richard Norton-Taylor[56] reported that as a result of the Lakenheath case a confidential official memo, leaked by a 'mole' at Menwith Hill, reveals that the Ministry of Defence complained to the US Embassy and the Third Air Force representatives about their handling of protestors entering US bases. The US was warned against repeating their aggressive action and told that since trespass is not an offence, any attempt to blindfold and handcuff a protestor could result in three months' imprisonment. The vice-commander of the USAF, according to this article, responded that he did not agree that such action constituted assault, raising a key question as to whether the US military is competent to decide on matters of English law or whether only an English court can decide on this. The eventual outcome of this case was that the US issued a Certificate of Immunity from Prosecution to prevent it from coming to court.

The evasion or simple ignoring of requests for information from public bodies revealed in this case raise some serious questions of democratic accountability, not only of US forces. Heather Brooke[57], an investigative journalist and Freedom of Information campaigner, who was responsible for uncovering the MPs expenses issue in 2008, makes this assessment of cultural attitudes among staff in publicly funded bodies in Britain. 'A faceless wall of bureaucracy has been built up that alienates the citizen from the state. If public servants are truly working for the public, then we need to know who they are... information collected in the name of the public expense belongs to the people, not to the bureaucracy'[58]. 'Deference and patronage still rule the day: [these issues] all grow from a single tragic belief; that the public can't be trusted. The corollary is that the state can. History shows the opposite is true: that individuals on their own do less damage than individuals hidden behind the walls of a faceless institution'[59]. And, finally, 'It is the people who give public servants their power, and so it must be the people to whom they are accountable, directly and forthrightly, with no middlemen in between'[60].

Case Study 3: The role and accountability of the Ministry of Defence Police (MODP)

The cases also led the campaigners to question the role and accountability of the Ministry of Defence Police Agency. An uncritical assumption by most British citizens would be that a civilian coming into contact with them would be safeguarded by the same laws, procedures and regulations which govern local police forces and with the same rights of complaint and appeal. They would also assume that they would be protected by them against unlawful behaviour from any source. The following information on the Ministry of Defence police is available from the MOD website.

The Ministry of Defence Police and Guarding Agency (MDGPA) was created in 1995, joining the civilian UK military police force (MODP) with the civilian Military Guarding Service (MGS). Its role is defined as 'delivering effective Policing and Guarding as part of the UK's defence capability' and its staff provide unarmed guarding access control services to MOD units across the UK, guarding over 200 sites including Faslane in Scotland, Menwith Hill and Fylingdales in North Yorkshire. Wikipedia states that although officially unarmed, '75% of MDGP staff on duty are armed at any one time'. As part of the regular MDGP police there are two further groups: the Territorial Support group, a specialist unit with advanced fire arms capability, which is available for response to threats to Atomic Weapons Establishments, and the Divisional Support Group comprising two mobile units (covering north and south regions) which provides rapid response to security or terrorist threats. Although MOD police take the same oath on appointment as local police, there are significant differences in their lines of accountability. Whereas police forces are locally based and accountable to elected Police Authorities, the MOD police are directly responsible to Whitehall, with no independent inspectorate. Their powers were significantly changed under the Armed Forces Act of 2001. They now have the powers to search and arrest any citizen and to deal with strikers, protestors and demonstrators. In effect this means that legal strikes and protests can be dealt with by armed military police, acting outside military areas. Nick Cohen,[61] argued that this is a significant breach of the principle that the military is under civilian control, and that civilians are likewise free from military control.

At the local level, the MDPGA enters into agreement with local Chief Constables to establish how they work together on securing local MOD sites. CAAB (see newsletter 41, 2009) asked for access to the protocol of understanding between the MDPGA and North Yorkshire Police concerning the bases at MHS and Fylingdales, using the Freedom of Information Act, but found that crucial sections were blacked out, especially those sections relating to the extent of the jurisdiction of the Agency.

How does the MDPGA work with US security forces on US bases in Britain? This is governed by the Memorandum of Agreement between the MOD (UK) and the US Air Force in Europe, represented by the HQ Third Air Force, of 2008, which addresses the provision of security and policing by the MDGPA to US forces in Britain. The terms of this agreement are available on the MOD website. In terms of accountability, the MDGPA officers are controlled, on US bases, by the US Base Commander for internal security tasks, but for the exercise of their constabulary powers outside the base they are responsible to the local senior MDGPA police officer who exercises tactical control. Overall operational control rests with the Chief Constable for the MOD police. All costs relating to the MDGPA (salaries, clothing, weapons, administration costs) are met by the US. The Director of Security on site (US) exercises operational control over the

MDGPA. For operations on site they are responsible to the US Director of Security. The role of the RAF Liaison Officer on US bases is described as being to ensure that liaison takes place between MDGPA and US personnel on sites and for monitoring and auditing practice.

The definition of the powers of the MDGPA as set out in this Memorandum of Understanding proved to be controversial. It states that while their full constabulary powers derive from the MDGPA Act of 1987, they also have powers under the Anti Terrorism, Crime and Security Act of 2001 to 'combat principal risks of crime and disorder faced by the MOD and the US Force'. Nick Cohen in the article cited above questions the extension of MDGPA powers over civilians and notes the danger of their possible use in times of legal strikes and civil protest. 'The absence of any debate about the powers of the MOD police ignores a basic principle of a free society that civilians are free from military control'. CAAB made a submission in 1999 to the House of Commons Select Committee expressing concern about the role of MDGPA police on US bases.

During the years of campaigning by CAAB significant questions and problems have emerged about the role of MDGPA police and how they work with US security staff. Clarification of their powers and accountability gradually became clear, both through Parliamentary questions and through court cases. What did the activities of CAAB reveal about the actual workings of the MDGPA in relation to peace protestors on US bases in Britain, and why did this become a focus for concern?

The two main activities of CAAB campaigners, which have brought them into contact with MDGPA police, are entering the bases to protest or to test the bye-laws (see above) and exercising the right of peaceful protest outside the bases. The RAF Croughton case already described shows what can happen when the protestors confronted both the MDGPA police and US security forces. US instructions under the Memorandum of Agreement are that if the intruder is British, MDGPA officers should deal with them. Significantly, in this case they did not choose, or were not allowed, to intervene even when Lindis Percy was body-searched. At her trial, the judge ruled that Lindis Percy had not been warned by the Senior Police Officer at the scene. As outlined above, part of the focus of the subsequent case by Lindis Percy against the officers involved in the incident was on the conduct and accountability of the US security Forces, but how do we explain the conduct of the MDGPA police?

The court proceedings of the Croughton Case at Northampton in 2006 give a real insight into the personal and professional responses and dilemmas of the MDGPA police. Under cross- examination one recalled that when he arrived at the scene, Lindis Percy was already handcuffed and surrounded by four, later five or six, US military personnel. The MDGPA asserted his authority and asked the US security officer to remove the handcuffs, who refused, saying he 'would go to jail if he did'. The police officer said he had no personal dealings with Lindis Percy but had heard of her actions over the years. Surprisingly he said he did not know that US authorities on a base can detain an intruder, but that if the intruder is a UK citizen then he or she must be handed over to the MDGPA as soon as is safe and practicable. His colleague, with 28 years of service in the force, knew of this but did not want to 'push this with the US military personnel'. As he was the senior officer, he should have served the section 69 notice, but neither officer knew this and the case was dismissed on a technicality.

The focus on this case as described above was on the conduct of the US personnel. But how do we explain the behaviour of the MDGPA? We know that no action was taken internally. Why was the Crown Prosecution Service concerned that the case should not come to court? What operational freedom really operates when the salaries and operational command of some aspects of the role of the MDGPA police are given to another organisation with probably different aims, values and culture? To whom did the MDGPA police present at that incident think they were accountable? It is arguable that the operational and support system within which MDGPA police operate contains the potential for confusion, divisions and marginalisation, to which we have to add questions about how peaceful protestors are viewed by the MDGPA police and their US pay-masters. Some indication is given in Lynn Smith's study of protest against war[62]. The US commander at the former US base at Greenham Common, when asked why he thought the protestors were there, replied in some perplexity that 'Some just [could] not have anything else in their lives', and saw them merely as a 'nuisance factor'.

What happens at the formal regular protests held outside the bases or at particular focussed demonstrations such at the annual July 4 demonstration? A recent development has been for the MDGPA police to read out to protestors at Menwith Hill, at the beginning of demonstrations, a Briefing Note which sets out where they may stand in relation to access and vehicle movement, stating the law under which arrests may take place if not adhered to (ie. under Obstruction of the Highways Act of 1988, and 'other legislation as appropriate'). There have also been instances where the MDGPA police have been effective in upholding the rights of peaceful protestors. In 2009, at Lakenheath, Lindis Percy demonstrated outside the main gate, holding the US flag upside down. The MDGPA police, supported by the Suffolk police and the station RAF Commander upheld her right of peaceful protest against US security forces. The US forces had initially responded with a 'lock down' of the base that lasted two hours, which was lifted when the local police arrived.

Earlier instances give a sense of the atmosphere and processes at CAAB protests. At one of the regular weekly protests held outside Menwith Hill in 2009, a handful of demonstrators, accompanied by some children, took advantage of the summer sunshine to hold a barbeque outside the main gate. They were met by three Divisional Support Group officers who are always present at the demonstration, along with 10 MDGPA police, three with semi-automatic weapons, and two guard dogs. The demonstration passed off peacefully but on the way back one demonstrator with a young child was followed along the A59 by MDGPA police who stopped her under the SOCPA of 2005. No offence had been committed and the police said it was a random stop.

In 2008 Lindis Percy was charged at Harrogate Magistrates' Court with obstructing the Highway while protesting at MHS on the fifth anniversary of the invasion of Iraq. She was arrested by officers of the MDGPA and of North Yorkshire Police, both being part of the counter-terrorist unit patrolling MHS. In the past CAAB had successfully resisted arrest under this Act citing the Hirst v Agu case of 1986, which laid down a clear legal precedent establishing that the 'lawful use' of the highway is not restricted to right of passage but covers other forms of activity such as protest. It allows protestors, especially in low key or moderate demonstrations to obstruct the highway if it is judged reasonable in the circumstances (the 'de minimus' clause), taking into account the length of the demonstration, its time and purpose. The case was dismissed, but on seven occasions at the weekly demonstrations Lindis Percy was arrested than released without charge when the demonstration had ended. This use by the police of a variety of laws, even when they had previously failed to gain a conviction, raises serious questions about the citizen's right to peaceful protest and to legal redress for wrongful arrest. The two strands of the court campaign that are outlined so far lead us to ask the question that is fundamental to the campaign: to whom are the US bases in Britain accountable both for the purposes to which they are put and for the policies and behaviour of their personnel?

The evidence from the campaign leads to the conclusion that the history, legal basis and continued agreements surrounding their use are surrounded in secrecy that is willingly backed by successive governments, and which is revealed only piecemeal by the persistent activities of campaigners through the methods outlined above. The central argument of CAAB, which it has developed over the twenty years or so of its campaign, is that US forces in the UK rest on unchallenged secret agreements, are largely unaccountable to the UK parliament for their use and function, and that the English legal system largely fails to protect UK citizens who challenge their function. It is possible to argue, as the responses to parliamentary questions have done repeatedly and as many would agree, that this is a reasonable price to pay for the protection and shared intelligence which the UK gains from this arrangement. However, there have been some alarming and unforeseen by-products of these informal agreements and of the secrecy which surrounds them.

In 1956 a potentially serious accident involving US aircraft at Lakenheath led to an evacuation of the base, and of the base at nearby Mildenhall, but local residents and the police were not informed. A year later, in 1957, John Foster Dulles made clear that no country with US bases had the right to veto the use of nuclear weapons. In effect this contradicted the original informal treaty of 1950 between the US and the UK about the right of the British government to control what happens on US bases in Britain. In May 1960, the US spy plane that was shot down over Russia was subsequently revealed to have left from Lakenheath without the knowledge of the British government. In 1973 Edward Heath prevented the US from using British airfields in Cyprus during the Yom Kippur war. In retaliation, Kissinger suspended intelligence-sharing for a week. Perhaps one of the most revealing episodes in US/UK relations is the secret depopulation of the island of Diego Garcia between 1965 and 1971. The British Foreign Office received $14 million and in return the US set up a major base for signals intelligence which, as recent Wiki leaks suggest was also used for staging flights for redaction of suspects during the 'War against Terror'. The legality of the forcible rendition from the UK of British subjects to prisons abroad for questioning, using methods illegal under English law, has been challenged in parliament and by lawyers in other countries.

Case Study 4: The 'American flag' cases and the 'Claim against the construction of two radomes at Menwith Hill'

These two cases provide an interesting counter-point to the prolonged bye-law cases. They are shorter and focus more clearly on issues relating to the interface of English and US law in relation to US bases in Britain, and on what can be achieved when a British citizen challenges important defence innovations on which there has been no public debate.

The 'American flag case' relates to two non-violent protests both carried out by Lindis Percy, first at RAF Feltwell in 2000 and secondly at Menwith Hill in the same year. In December 2000, in protest against the use US Missile Defence System, Lindis Percy used the US flag as a visual means of demonstrating this protest. She placed a stripe against the stars on the flag and wrote 'Stop Star Wars' across the stars holding the flag, stepped in front of vehicles leaving the base, displaying the flag and attempting to engage with the occupants of the vehicles in discussion of the reasons behind her action. Initially Lindis Percy was charged under the *Crime and Disorder Act of 1986* for committing a racially aggravated offence, but this charge was dropped and instead she was charged with Obstruction of the Highway and under *section 5 of the Public Order Act of 1980* for 'using threatening, abusive or insulting words or behaviour likely to cause harassment, alarm or distress'. At the subsequent hearing at Fakenham County Court in Norwich (after the arrest at

Feltwell), in May 2011, the District Judge found Lindis guilty on both counts, fining her £200 for the Public Order offence and £100 for obstructing the highway. He made it clear that in his view there was no breach of the Human Rights Act and in particular stressed the need for sensitivity in a multi-cultural society to the significance of cultural symbols. This decision was appealed on the grounds that flag denigration is a form of protest renowned world-wide, which is afforded protection in other jurisdictions, including in the US itself. At a hearing in December 2001 at the Queen's Bench Divisional Court, Mrs. Justice Hallett quashed the Fakenham conviction. She commented particularly on *sections 5 and 6 of the Public Order Act* which specifically provided for the defence of reasonableness and contained a necessary balance between the right to freedom of expression and the right of others not to be insulted or distressed. She asked whether in this case the use of the defendant's own property to convey a lawful message was reasonable and whether in this case the state's response to interfere with that freedom was proportionate. In this hearing the judges found in that Lindis Percy's defence that her actions were part of her lawful right to freedom of expression under *Article 10 of the ECHR* had been given insufficient weight by the District Judge and therefore the conviction was quashed.

In the second instance Lindis Percy engaged in December 2000 in a similar protest at Menwith Hill. Disturbed by the recent election of George Bush as US president, given his known views on the development of the US Missile Defense programme, she took a US flag within the main gate at Menwith Hill, this time causing delay to vehicles leaving the base. Again she was charged under the *CJPO*

Act of 1994 with racially aggravated 'abusive or insulting behaviour', namely trailing a US flag on the ground in front of cars driven by American citizens within sight of persons likely to be caused distress or harassment thereby' and 'motivated by hostility towards members of the USA based on their membership of that group'. There is no video evidence for the charge of trailing the flag. The charge of racial motivation was later dropped, but under *section 5 of the Public Order Act of 1980* Lindis Percy was charged additionally with 'abusive and insulting behaviour as well as the original charge of obstructing the highway'. The CPS prepared in evidence 17 handwritten statements taken by the MDPA which included accounts from 10 Americans of their experience of the protest.

The case was heard at Harrogate Magistrates' Court in April 2001 before District Judge Peter Nuttall. Lindis was by then represented by a London-based firm of solicitors and by a barrister, Rajiv Menon. In introducing his defence of Lindis Percy he stated his opinion that 'we would not be here today if it was not for a highly politically motivated prosecution'. He also drew to the attention of the court the fact that the US Supreme Court had refused to make flag abuse a criminal offence. Lindis Percy was found not guilty of obstructing the highway and in addition, she was found not guilty of the charges under the Criminal Justice and Public Order Acts. Judge Nuttall largely dismissed the witness statements collected by the CPS, noting that 75% of them had not found Lindis Percy's behaviour insulting and stating that the evidence of 'three American zealots' was 'completely over the top'. The judge criticised the MDPA for asking anyone on the base if they were offended by Lindis' actions, obviously a leading question. 'We do have rights as citizens and they include the right to protest. Nobody could say that this was other than a peaceful protest'. Judge Nuttall also concluded that he doubted that charges needed to have been made within the criminal code.

These two cases, like those described earlier in the bye-laws account, are again important in their implications for civil liberties and the right to peaceful protest. They demonstrate again the success of one campaigner, acting as a private citizen in obtaining decisive judgements both at local courts and in High Court hearings. These judgements gave unequivocal priority to the rights of individuals to freedom of expression as defined by the ECHR, and represent an unwillingness to use legislation primarily aimed at addressing criminal or lawless behaviour to stop peaceful protest.

The case of the Claim (in English legal terminology 'writ') **against the erection of two radomes** at Menwith Hill is distinctive in that it is a legal challenge by the two campaigners, acting as private individuals, against named individuals from the US military, and from the British defence establishment, who had clear areas of responsibility for what happened at Menwith Hill. The challenge has a definitely quixotic quality. In October 1999 Lindis Percy noticed that contractors' equipment was being moved onto the site where two new SBIRS radomes were to be built. Lindis Percy then quickly assembled a Claim to stop these being built on the written grounds that such action would violate local, national and international law (in the latter case specifically the ABM treaty of 1972, and the Outer Space Treaty of 1969) and sought a High Court injunction to restrain the agents from starting construction. This claim was issued in the High Court in London against four named defendants.

1. Colonel D Harthcock, the US Commander at Menwith Hill.

2. The Secretary of State for Defence, as the possessor of the land at Menwith Hill.

3. The Defence Land Agent, who acts on behalf of the American client for planning applications and developments at Menwith Hill.

4. Squadron Leader H. Vincent, the RAF Liaison Officer at Menwith Hill.

In the second stage of the action, Colonel Harthcock, represented by a major law firm, Clifford Chance, asked for an extension of time in order to allow him to consult with the US government. This was granted, as were similar applications by the three other defendants.

In the third stage defendants 2, 3 and 4 asked for the claim to be 'struck out' on the grounds that the claim was an abuse of court and that British courts had no jurisdiction in this case.

This was not granted.

In January 2000 the case was heard in Chambers before Master Tennant. By then Lindis Percy was represented with legal aid, and statements on her behalf were made to the hearing by Professor Paul Rogers from the Bradford Department of Peace Studies, and by Professor N Grief from Bournemouth University. Master Tennant suggested that the claim be amended and that preliminary costs of £4,500 be awarded against Lindis Percy, to be paid before any further action was taken. It is surprising, and a measure of the interest and support generated by this case, that this sum was raised by donations within two weeks. Colonel Harthcock then applied for 'state immunity' and costs against Lindis Percy, the request being granted in July 2000.

In stage 4, the claim was amended to include Fylingdales and the case was scheduled to be heard in open chambers by a High Court Judge in October 2000. Defendants 2, 3 and 4 were to be represented by an expert in international law from London University. However, before the arguments could be heard in open court, in a parallel development President Clinton agreed to put the development of the NMD system 'on hold' until after the US presidential elections in November 2000. After a conference, Lindis Percy accepted legal advice to withdraw her claim. Defendants 2, 3 and 4 were awarded costs against Lindis of £11,000.

What was the value to CAAB of this short and rather inconclusive action?

It established that the British officials could not claim that the case could not be heard in an English court. It established that a private citizen could call them to account to explain their actions in an open court before a judge. This would also have given CAAB the forum in which to state the reasons for their action.

It also repeated the lesson learnt in the 'Immunity of Visiting Forces' case that a high-ranking US officer could successfully claim immunity from appearing in an English court.

It demonstrated real interest and support not only from CAAB supporters but also in the media. This may be because clear and unequivocal action was being taken, which went to the heart of the defence agreements between the US and UK governments, and which, if pursued, would have brought into open public debate the local, national and international implications of the arms race in space.

CAAB itself (see newsletter 16) said that the chief value to them had been that during the course of the legal action they had amassed more detailed information about the US Missile Defense System and international law. The case revealed that Menwith Hill was crucially connected with Missile Defense and this knowledge was available to a wider public after the prominence given to it in the media.

Acknowledging that these cases represent only a small part of CAAB's court campaign, it may be useful at this point to record what Lindis Percy sees as the court campaigns' important achievements. She says that 'after eight years of challenging the unprofessional and abusive way the MOD police behaved at the weekly Tuesday demonstration we finally achieved a situation whereby there has been a complete change of policy in the way the demonstration has been policed... I have continually challenged... and refused to accept what they have done (spurious arrests, attempts at ASBO, pushing the boundaries the police made up,) making many, many complaints, bringing private prosecutions, writing letters on behalf of CAAB, requesting endless meetings with senior officers of North Yorkshire Police and MOD police. In fact, knowing they were abusing their powers only made me challenge and confront what they were doing the more! 'Discovering how the MOD police are different from the Home Office police and challenging this even though they are dressed like Home Office police. Challenging the powers that they said they had but did not, obtaining with the help of MPs various Memoranda of Understanding which showed that they are paid and controlled by the US authorities, insisting that we have the right to protest and establishing this'. Martin Schweiger, (see interviews recorded later) says that the reduction of arrests on Tuesday evenings and the calmer approach taken has probably only come about because of Lindis Percy's court appearances. This is both more economical and a better use of police resources; it also makes more sense on the ground. Lindis also notes that after the years of testing the 'yellow line' the police do not now intervene or interfere. 'The North Yorkshire police got so fed up with me being endlessly arrested by the MOD...in fact they said so to me!' In general Lindis Percy also concludes that she has 'brought under public scrutiny and awareness, issues concerning US bases'.

She also says how shocked she was by many aspects of court procedure, especially where she believed that the police have lied on oath and where the courts have colluded with the police. Many of the cases in which she was involved were political cases and she has exposed obstruction and incompetence by the CPS. In general she feels that she has shown repeatedly how important it is to ask questions of those in authority, to challenge abuse of the law by the police especially in cases involving civil liberties, and to show how an ordinary citizen can act within the law to challenge practices that affect the fundamental liberties of us all.

Chapter 6

Peaceful Witness

It has become obvious during this analysis how far CAAB methods and activities have moved from the Greenham days of peace camps and of public demonstrations outside bases. However it is important to be aware that alongside the court campaigns and the careful elucidation of the nature and legality of US bases in Britain there is also an aspect to the campaign that can best be described as public witness and an effort to engage local and national public opinion regarding the issues at stake. These can be summarised as follows:

- The weekly demonstration outside Menwith Hill Station usually on Tuesdays between 6 and 8pm, now in its tenth year.

- Holding bi-monthly Quaker Meeting for Worship outside various US bases, including Menwith Hill.

- Holding an annual demonstration outside MHS on US Independence Day (July 4), called 'Independence from America' day and held every year since the early 1980's.

- Establishing links with academics, other campaigning groups with a similar focus both in the UK and world-wide, exchanging information, writing and delivering information papers, setting up and maintaining a web-site.

- Publication of a monthly news letter, and compiling regular reports on key current issues.

- Giving talks in the community, to colleges, schools, universities, religious bodies, community groups.

- Establishing links with local and national media and contributing to articles.

These aspects of CAAB will be described and enriched by comparing them with the activities and achievements of a campaign that is comparable in terms of its focus and methods. This is the Faslane 365 campaign in Scotland, which focuses on non-violent protest against the siteing of nuclear weapons at Faslane naval base. The Faslane peace camp and blockade of 2007 has some striking similarities with CAAB and, at the same time differences in organisation and scope of activities which provide a useful and interesting 'compare and contrast' exercise for peace campaigners.

The Faslane 365 blockade followed the 'Trident Ploughshares' campaign, which organised peace camps at Faslane and Coulport naval bases in Scotland as a witness against nuclear weapons, particularly Trident. In 2007 this peace camp celebrated 25 years and became the longest-running peace camp in Britain. Faslane 365 aimed to organise a year-round blockade of the bases in order to revitalise the campaign and to raise again in public and political consciousness the key arguments against nuclear weapons. The experiences of that year and the issues raised are strikingly similar to those of CAAB. Notably, these are: the principled adherence to non-violent protest, the ideological inheritance from the Greenham campaign, and the growing awareness of the need to move away from this activity and to embrace new forms of protest. Their fundamental argument is that public protest is not enough, and that arrests and public arguments in the courts make the concern both visible and clearly articulated, which in turn can be powerful in bringing about social change. The court campaign which developed from this approach led to similar experiences with the local police and the MOD police, and encountered a similar use of different legal means to silence peaceful protest. Faslane 365 also struggled to engage local and national opinion with the issues involved through engagement with academics, the media and national politicians, and gave serious attention to analysis, debate and education in the understanding and exposure of the existence of nuclear weapons.

However there are important differences between the two campaigns. The scale of the Faslane blockade is far wider and was clearly successful in engaging groups and individuals from across Britain who had not previously been engaged in non-violent protest. Perhaps relevant to this is the nature and extent of the organisation. While avowedly non-hierarchical, it is plainly more extensive than the small numbers actively involved with CAAB. The political climate in which the campaigns operated is markedly different. Zelter[63] noted the different attitudes of the Scottish press and political opinion towards the presence of nuclear submarines at Faslane and contrasted this with the environment of Greenham and Aldermaston where she noted that there appeared to be no local criticism of the defence establishment. This is also relevant to the situation of both Menwith Hill and Fylingdales, both located in rural North Yorkshire, which (with the occasional exception of Harrogate), has returned a Conservative MP for most of the twentieth and twenty-first centuries. Perhaps the most fundamental difference between the two campaigns is that Faslane is a UK Navy base, and not a US base so that the range of issues of sovereignty and accountability which arise from this are not present. What follows is an attempt to summarise some of the activities of Faslane 365, to note what they themselves judged to be significant and effective, and where they felt they had been less successful.

In a clear parallel with CAAB's court campaigns (but allowing for differences in Scottish law), the campaigners challenged the actions of the police in their responses to legal, non-violent protests. Over the whole year of the campaign, in which 131 blockading groups covered 188 days, there were 1150 arrests, of which 75 proceeded to prosecution. Of these, there were 33 convictions, and 28 were acquitted (14 were still being heard at the time of publication of the book (2008)). The organisers argued that the use of arrest and overnight imprisonment without the intention to proceed to prosecution is a breach of the ECHR Act which states this is illegal. They also argued that since Trident was illegal in international law, their non violent protests could not be judged to be illegal. As with the experience of CAAB, they found that, in order to evade testing these arguments in court, the police had to find other grounds for arrest, for example Breach of the Peace. In common with CAAB they also noted the different responses between the local Strathclyde police, with whom they established channels of communication and dialogue, and the MOD police with whom they experienced higher levels of tension and perceived some rivalry with the local police. This is in a situation where there is no added complication of the relations with the US security forces or the accompanying problems of financial control and divided accountability.

The Faslane campaign engaged very seriously in debates about the role of academic institutions in working towards a vision of a society free from nuclear weapons, and one in which democratic debate and accountability are reclaimed and safeguarded. In an impressive range of papers given in the blockade seminars, there was exploration not only of global issues concerning local livelihoods, eco-systems and the current economic crisis, but also what is happening in academia today. How far are the military and financial intersts involved in research directed towards their own interests, and how can the academic world be a force for peace and social change? The impact on universities of the audit culture and of management control were also discussed.

Paul Rogers, in his introduction to the Faslane account, stressed the importance of the contribution that Faslane 365 made not only to the arguments against nuclear power, but also in its challenge to 'old thinking' about global security. In his opinion, it is more than an anti nuclear witness that empowers the people involved and introduces a new generation to non violent action, 'it also revitalises a critically important debate'[64]. Again, echoing the arguments of CAAB, he added, 'nuclear weapons do not exist in a vacuum... they exist in a web of lies, evasions and power abuses and the success of both campaigns lies partly in their exposure of the institutions and structures that sustain and underpin nuclear and militarily defined approaches to security'[65].

In retrospect, the Faslane campaigners were self-critical of aspects of their campaigning. They did not feel they were always sensitive in their relations with local people and with citizens employed at the bases. They acknowledged the temptation to be patronising and not to engage with how locals saw and experienced the campaign. Gradually they developed structures for facilitating communication and grew to understand the need to work on a respectful understanding of the police, the security services and those who worked at Faslane. They stressed the importance of developing a non-violent vocabulary in describing those who work in the nuclear industry, and of engaging with their real knowledge, experiences and their fears about their job security and the local economy. This insight took the campaigners back to the first principles of non-violence, 'that there is a connectedness between each of us as individuals and every other part of nature... our language must not deny this.'[66]. For the Menwith Hill campaigners, the temptation to see as 'other' those who do not share their vision and values is, perhaps, increased by the fact that many of those with whom they come into direct contact were from the US military, or employed by them, and largely male. Feelings of patriotism, awareness of cultural and political differences, and anger at current foreign and military policies can all contribute to a polarisation of attitudes. Conversely, for people who do not share the expressed values of opposition to nuclear weapons or to non-violence, a sense at both local and national levels of gratitude to the US, of shared cultural and historical references of 'facing a common danger' all contribute to a readiness to accept, or preparedness to ignore, the security and constitutional problems raised by nuclear weapons and by the place of US bases in Britain.

Community focussed activities

This phrase is used to cover activities carried out by CAAB which are broadly aimed at engaging with and informing, local people and organisations with the purpose both of sharing information and stimulating informed discussion of the issues of US bases in Britain. This includes monitoring local planning applications, using traditional forms of protest such as vigils and silent demonstrations, establishing relationships with journalists, other peace bodies, academics and local and national politicians, and giving talks and lectures to local groups.

Monitoring local planning applications

This proved to be an effective method of gaining and spreading local information. A named person initially undertook a weekly monitoring of planning applications submitted to Harrogate Planning offices relating to MHS and Fylingdales. Now this can be done using the Local Authority website. Local procedures require that if more than seven objections are received to an application, it may then go to the Area Planning sub-committee, which is open to the public and where objectors can speak for up to three minutes. CAAB found it useful to work with local councillors on the Planning Committee. The importance of this activity became apparent in 1997, when four planning applications for more radomes and support buildings at MHS received thirteen objections. One councillor was troubled at the encroachment on land, bringing it closer to the A59. He asked what would happen if the council rejected the application and was given legal advice that it would go back to the Ministry of Defence, who would appeal to the Secretary of State for Defence, who would approve it. This undermining of local democracy is not surprising to environmental campaigners, for example, when opposing the siting of supermarkets in or near small communities, but it is perhaps rare in spelling out so clearly the limitations placed on local planners and on local accountability.

Earlier, in 1995, an application to Harrogate Planning Department for two eighty foot CCTV masts for security cameras on the outer limits of MHS was objected to by the local council because of their visual intrusion in an Area of Outstanding Natural Beauty. The Council was told that they had no power to reject a Crown Planning Application and that the MOD was the authorising authority and not the Local Authority. The frustration of local councillors was shown in a BBC 'Look North' programme when one councillor described their impotence in this case and themselves as 'dummies' paid for at the ratepayers' expense.

Perhaps the clearest vindication of this area of CAAB's work came in 1997 when the preparation for the new radomes was noticed and there was a growing realisation on the part of the campaigners that there was to be significant development at MHS. This led to a long and costly attempt by Lindis Percy to obtain a High Court injunction to stop the development on the grounds that it breached international law (the 1972 ABM treaty and the 1967 Outer Space Treaty). This led to questions in the Houses of Lords and Commons on the legality of the operations and on the powers of the local planning authority in relation to MHS. Paul Rogers (op cit) regarded this action by CAAB as an important contribution to the awareness of the UK government's early decision to support the US in the 'Star Wars' project and to starting the debate about is legality and effectiveness. Monitoring the planning applications also yielded information about the weakness of Health and Safety regulations relating to the disposal of hazardous waste at MHS, of threats to local flora and fauna, and to the rights of access for disabled people.

Traditional forms of silent protest, vigils and demonstrations

These have, in CAAB's case, taken the form of regular Quaker Meetings for Worship and silent vigils held outside the base at Menwith Hill. In addition special demonstrations have been held on July 4 (US Independence Day) every year, and also at times of crisis, either international or over particular issues. For example, CAAB cooperated with CND in an event on March 4 2000 when more than 400 people came to Menwith Hill to protest against SBIRS, and letters of support were read from similar campaigns against US bases in New Zealand, Canada, Germany and the Pacific Islands. In July 2000, again supported by Yorkshire CND, 50 people attended a 'Public Declaration of Independence from America' at Menwith Hill, followed by a 60 mile walk

117

to Fylingdales, where around 130 people protested against Fylingdale's role in the NMD system.

Sharing and disseminating information
CAAB records demonstrate the importance attached by the campaigners to the sharing of information gathered and elicited by them with Peace groups in the UK and abroad, and with academics, such as those in the local Peace Studies Department at Bradford University. This small campaign received and shared information, and maintained a significant profile in wider debates and issues on which their activities had shed a sometimes small but significant light even when they were not central to the campaign, writing papers to public committees and other bodies for example the House of Commons Joint Committee on Human Rights, and to the House of Commons Defence Committee. There is substantial documentation of the background to these papers in the CAAB records.

Engagement with local groups
A quick overview of these activities gleaned from CAAB newsletters covering just one year of the campaign (2007) revealed the following engagement with community groups and organisations:

> Eleven talks (to schools, CND conference, Leeds University, 'Stop the War Coalition'.)

Nineteen interviews with the Press and radio (New Statesman, Look North, BBC Radio Leeds).

This range of activities is a more traditional and relatively uncontroversial form of non-violent protest. Essentially it has as its focus raising public awareness of issues that are either hidden, not discussed publicly or framed in terms of an unquestioning acceptance of official versions and received opinions. It allows participation by campaigners who are not drawn to, or may honestly feel unable to cope with the demands made by direct action as described in this account. The next chapter describes the personal costs of this campaign in more detail.

Chapter 7

Towards evaluation: voices from inside and outside the campaign

It is possible to see CAAB's activities to date as encompassing two distinct strands. Mendel (71) characterised these as, on the one hand 'the prophetic vocation of non-violence' which cannot be judged by contemporary standards of success, and on the other the 'reconcilers' who 'work within the established system to lay the foundations of a better world'. Mendel did not see these as mutually exclusive, arguing rather that the most effective campaigns contain both elements with all the accompanying tensions. It is clear from the analysis so far that CAAB contains both these strands of activity. The values which underlie the peaceful witness are close to a 'prophetic' stance, although one does not need to be a Quaker or to have religious convictions to follow this path. It can be argued that the prophetic stance has its own justification in that it witnesses to a truth about the human condition, opposing accepted wisdom such as slavery or the denial of equality to women, which may take generations to change, but where the truth must be publicly declared so that the evil or injustice is not allowed to go unchallenged. This is an underlying aspect to the CAAB campaign, which is fundamental to its values and methods of campaigning.

Paul Rogers considered that one of the strengths of CAAB has been its clear focus on the key issue of the accountability of US bases in Britain, and raising awareness of the dangers and risks to Britain of their presence. This has led the campaign into legal and political confrontation, and it is this aspect of CAAB's campaign that is more open to evaluation, and which is addressed in this chapter. The following approaches have been adopted in attempting to summarise and evaluate the achievements of CAAB as set out in this research. First, a series of interviews with outside individuals who provide valuable insights into how the campaign has been perceived; secondly, interviews with the two main campaigners to hear their assessment of their work and, finally, a reflection on the campaign employing tools from the field of conflict analysis and resolution.

With one exception, all those interviewed were broadly sympathetic to the campaign. The voices of those who challenge what the campaign is trying to do, and particularly those who believe strongly in what might be described as traditional answers to international and domestic problems, such as valuing a nuclear military defence and a close alliance with the US, are absent. The viewpoints of the US base commanders at Menwith Hill, of the RAF liaison officers, and of the MDGPA are not heard. All were asked for an interview and all (courteously) declined. It was therefore particularly valuable to talk to Wing Commander Mick Marsh, who, although with no personal knowledge of CAAB, nevertheless as RAF Liaison Officer at Greenham Common in the 1980s could give valuable insights into the impact of a different sort of non-violent protest on a military base.

The lawyer

Mark Stephens is a lawyer who in the early years of the campaign acted as legal representative for Lindis Percy. Keir Starmer (Director of Public Prosecutions 2008 to 2013) was the barrister in the same London practice at the time. Mark Stephens called this period of his practice 'cutting our teeth on the Lindis Percy cases'. His assessment of CAAB is that it was a very significant campaign which has a lasting legacy. Its importance, he believes, lies in two significant contributions. The first is illustrated by the bye-laws campaign which he believes was the first to adopt the tactic of challenging the law while staying within it. The aim of this tactic was to clarify the law, for example by taking the bye-law signs down but not stealing them. This meant that the cases came back to court to test the legality of displaying the signs but with no option for the prosecution of making a criminal charge against the protestors. The second lasting legacy, he argues, lies in the fact that most NGOs now employ lawyers as a matter of course. Mark Stephens himself now acts as legal adviser to Greenpeace and says that he is 'building on the legacy of the Lindis Percy cases'.

In his opinion the campaign marked a sea-change in the area of peaceful protest and challenged the notion that the police and legal system could criminalise peace protestors and other campaigners. In retrospect he says it is a campaign 'of which he is most proud'. Mark Stephens also gave his opinion on issues that arose during the campaign and which are discussed earlier in this paper. They concern not the methods of the campaign but its contribution to facts about US bases in Britain. He believes that there is clear evidence that there was communication between US and

British authorities concerning how Lindis Percy should be dealt with, especially when the different legal pretexts for arresting her and prohibiting her from entering US bases failed to hold up in court. He also commented on the long running contact between the campaigners and the MOD police. He observed that when the campaigners challenged the US but still acted within the law (for example making a citizen's arrest of a US officer carrying a gun on an English highway) the MOD police were often at a loss as to how to proceed, possibly because their training did not include dealing with peaceful protestors, and frequently therefore Lindis would be tried but acquitted because legal technicalities had not been observed. Mark Stephens concluded, 'this is a very important campaign, its legacy must not be lost'.

The Parliamentarians

(These opinions were recorded before the Edward Snowden revelations and before the new restrictions on the allowed scope of parliamentary questions in 2013 already referred to).

Baroness Sue Miller, a Liberal Democratic peer in the House of Lords, expressed considerable respect for the work of CAAB. As a parliamentarian, she believes that the posing of properly framed parliamentary questions is vital in connecting parliament to its grass roots. The questions and the background to the questions provided by CAAB give Members of both Houses of Parliament information that they can then take up with ministers and civil servants. This continual challenge is, in her opinion, vital if we are not to slide into a police state. She expressed her own sense of powerlessness to change things and her feelings of perplexity about what she called 'kowtowing to the US', asking what pressures are exerted by them and who actually benefits most from 'the special relationship'.

In terms of personalities, Baroness Miller sees Lindis Percy as essentially a credible campaigner given her background as a midwife and her life experience as a mother and grandmother. In her opinion Lindis 'strikes a chord' with parliament when she focuses on civil liberties, but less so when emphasising the pacifist and disarmament aspects of the campaign. She praised the skill of the campaign in its relationship with the press and advised that the use of parliamentary questions be vigorously pursued in the (then) new parliament.

Fabian Hamilton (MP Leeds North East) has asked many parliamentary questions on behalf of CAAB, and he describes this process as 'a very powerful tool'. In clarification of the procedures that have to be followed, he said that written questions are submitted according to a set format, and that they are not 'screened out' by any vetting committee, and have to be answered. As we have seen, these can sometimes produce only a limited response or can be refused on security grounds, but this in itself can be informative. He confirmed that MPs are not bound to submit questions when asked by their constituents and that therefore the importance to the campaign of identifying and working with sympathetic MPs is crucial.

In general, Fabian Hamilton considers that CAAB and similar campaigns are vital in a vibrant democracy in raising issues of accountability and freedom, for example we need to know who pays for US bases in Britain. However, he believes that the issue of US bases is not usually at the top of anyone's agenda and is unlikely to bring about any changes in government policy in the short or medium term.

The Academic

Paul Rogers is Professor of Peace Studies at Bradford University and has had both an academic and a personal involvement in non-violent campaigns across a wide spectrum of causes. He believes that the distinctive features of CAAB has been not only its steady focus and persistence over two decades but also the relative modesty of its aims in that it is not aiming at the abolition of US bases in Britain but at their accountability. Supporting the views of Mark Stephens, he believes that its success lies in providing the example for ordinary citizens to take legal action through the courts, in this way opening up important state documents in the face of obstruction and opposition. It has shown what knowledgeable and determined campaigners can do even when faced with formidable state power. Paul Rogers also believes that the campaigners' steady accumulation of accurate and well resourced information has been vital in empowering their campaign. In terms of the timing of the campaign he argues that it has been fortunate in that international events (the ending of the Cold War, wars in Iraq and Afghanistan) have fed public unease about US power and made questions particularly relevant about why Menwith Hill still stands and is expanding. An excellent example of the campaign's effectiveness was its ability to feed early into the whole debate about Missile Defence, due to their monitoring of what was happening at MHS. This added to the knowledge and awareness of campaigns with a similar focus (such as CND, the Arms trade campaign.)

In summary, Paul Rogers concluded: 'It is an enduring witness, a twenty year campaign of great value'.

The Journalists

It is obvious from the account of the campaign that the press and media have been of crucial importance in bringing its activities and the issues raised to a wider audience.

Richard Norton-Taylor is Security Editor for 'The Guardian' and has been in contact with CAAB since the early 1990s. His assessment of CAAB is that the information gathered by them over the years has been reliable and well researched, and has certainly revealed information not obtainable elsewhere. 'It is indeed a unique body'. Richard Norton-Taylor believes that its key contribution has been to put the spotlight onto US bases in Britain. 'In particular it has shown how the issue remains an important one and that the closing down of many former USAF bomber bases does not mean that the whole question of the US presence in Britain is not as important as at the height of the Cold War. 'Quite the contrary.'

He looks ahead to what he sees as possible ways forward for the campaign. He recommends the continuation and development of strong links with organisations and networks with similar aims (for example, CND and Stop the War Coalition), and extending its mailing list as much as possible. Above all he believes that keeping Missile Defense as a prominent issue is vital, since it is no longer high on the political agenda in Britain but, he believes, is still a huge issue in NATO, creating substantial arguments between the US and Russia. 'Continuing to disseminate and disclose information about what the US is up to here as soon as possible would be good'.

Peter Lazenby has been a reporter with the Yorkshire Post for over 30 years and has written about CAAB regularly. He regards CAAB as an excellent source of information on US bases in Britain, and on Menwith Hill in particular. From them, he received an overview of all the US Bases, how they were set up, and how parliamentary questions could be used to 'keep the government on the back foot'. Peter Lazenby finds the CAAB newsletter a reliable source of information, not only for the big stories but also for small items of information that can be used as the basis for a big story. He regards the campaign as a good model for other protest groups, excellent at all levels of action and 'one of the most reliable and consistent sources of information... a very important and principled campaign'.

The RAF Liaison Officer

From the interviews quoted so far, it is clear that the contributors, albeit from their own professional viewpoints, are broadly sympathetic to the aims and values of CAAB. It is therefore very valuable to hear viewpoints which derive from a different background and viewpoint. Wing Commander Mick Marsh was RAF Liaison Officer at Greenham Common Airbase between 1983 and 1986 and with his wife Ann, contributed the following valuable insights into the life of an RAF officer holding a position in a US controlled airbase during a period of concentrated and prolonged protest against the placement of Cruise missiles on the site. This campaign, which started in 1980, became famous world- wide. It was based on women only peace camps located around the base. There are obvious major differences between this campaign and CAAB, and Wing Commander Marsh has no first-hand knowledge of the latter campaign. Nevertheless he and his wife were able to give insights into what life was like in a military base where personnel of different nationalities, cultures, military background and command structures had to find a way of responding to a form of protest that challenged the values and military justification of their presence there.

Wing Commander Marsh describes his role of RAF Commander as being one of liaison with the US military on Greenham and of ensuring that 'British standards were met'. He used the term of 'feeling like a tennis ball', and referred to his early awareness of issues of relative power that existed between US and RAF personnel. It was seen as important that his ranking be set at the equivalent of US Colonel and he felt that the presence on the base, for a time, of an RAF regiment and of two battalions of British soldiers affected perceptions of his status and power. Both he and Ann Marsh described Greenham as 'Little America', and had no doubt that there were important cultural differences, for example over respect for English law. Ann described a social meeting with US army wives when she had to speak forcefully for the rights of the women to protest. 'It is a free country, my father was in the last war, the women are doing what they think is right to protect their children, my children, your children'[67]. She and Mick both humorously acknowledged the remarks made by a US officer, perhaps jokingly, about the wish to behave to the protestors as they would were they on a US base in countries where the right to protest was not safeguarded in law, and of the expressed perplexity and intense frustration that the women could get away with trespassing on the base, even when they were acting within the law.

Wing Commander Marsh conveyed a sense of the difficulties experienced on all sides when in the presence of protestors. For most of the US soldiers there it was the first time that they had been overseas, and his experience was that they were watched carefully in their contact with protestors. 'Those who were untrustworthy were excluded or sent home', although this is not clear whether 'untrustworthy' refers to a lack of respect for English law (as the CAAB campaigners encountered) or a willingness to engage in conversation with the protestors. Wing Commander Marsh saw the MOD police as the men who had most day-to-day contact with the protestors, which again echoes the CAAB experience.

In conversation it was plain that the RAF Liaison Officer has a key role in liaising with the local community, setting up an Anglo/US committee that established links with local groups and bodies such as Rotary. A later RAF Commander at Greenham, Group Captain Stanley Keyte[68] says: 'The Americans would depend on me to keep them out of trouble. It was necessary to be quite firm with their troops. There were cultural differences, a wish on their part to take direct action, to go out there and get the women by the scruff of their neck'. Both Wing Commander Marsh and his wife echoed Wing Commander Keyte in saying that, in retrospect, the years at Greenham were frustrating but extremely satisfying: 'the best and most rewarding tour my wife and I had anywhere'.

A Quaker witness for peace

Martin Schweiger, Quaker and local Medical Officer for Environmental Health contributed to this evaluation from a viewpoint of having taken part over six years in the weekly Tuesday demonstrations outside Menwith Hill. He is therefore more detached from the ongoing activities of the two main campaigners, whose contributions are heard next.

Martin Schweiger clearly defined CAAB as a campaign that is rooted in the Quaker peace testimony and which, although not owned by the Society of Friends as a concern, deserves the support of Friends as do other campaigns such as Liberty or Amnesty. Personally, he has chosen to support the part of the campaign that is most important to him, the Meetings for Worship that witness to the spiritual basis of the work, and which also allow him to engage with the MDGPA officers, sometimes on health issues which concern them and their families, sometimes on the protest itself. He described occasions when, for example, the pupils of a local Quaker school, the Mount, attended the meeting for Worship, which encouraged the local MOD police to come out and talk to them about peaceful policing. For Martin Schweiger this emphasis on personal engagement with the military is a very important form of activity but different from more confrontational tactics that involve challenging the law. However he was in no doubt about the importance of the campaign in keeping the issue in the public eye over the decades, and in revealing the dangerous truths about what goes on in Menwith Hill which he describes as, 'increasingly a big and dangerous gun site'. In his opinion the campaign has revealed the political pressure that is brought to bear on the CPS and the ways in which big interests overwhelm democratic accountability, which have been glimpsed on the occasions when CAAB has 'plainly encountered very powerful interests'.

The Campaigners

This chapter ends with interviews with the two main campaigners. What follows is less an attempt to assess how they evaluate their own success than an opportunity to hear personal accounts which reflect on what they did and also, often unwittingly, reveals the personal cost that this long campaign has exacted in their lives.

Anni Rainbow

Anni Rainbow retired from active campaigning in 2006 due to health problems but retains the role of valued supporter, and is a source of history and reflection for the continuing campaigners. She talked of the sense that by the end of her time with the campaign it had 'taken over everything' in her life. She recalls definite feelings of fear in some of the face to face encounters with the US military, a feeling that physical violence towards protestors was more acceptable to them than to British police, followed by increasing frustration at what to her seemed obvious intervention in English court processes, in which she feels the US military perpetrators were not always found out. She described how she moved in her thinking and actions from initial protests about the Vietnam War to increasingly questioning the weapons used by the US military and then on to questioning the nature and status of US bases in Britain. She looks back to her own naivety about the bases and her growing awareness of the secrecy that surrounds them and their lack of accountability in English law. In particular she recalls her reaction to the Feltwell case (see above) when she realised that the MOD officer would not or could not protect a British subject on a US base against an armed US soldier. She says she was 'flabbergasted'. 'I am not really that patriotic, but it offends my sense of values, of truth and justice and what is important.' Anni recalled, too, some of her conversations with the MOD police and her sense that many do not want to think of the extent to which the US is in charge, and instead focus on their own structures. Asked if her opposition to US bases in Britain would be as strong, even if the issue of nuclear weapons was not involved, Anni's response was that it would, 'knowing how deviously they came into being and that there is no safety in English law from them. The more you find out, the more you know that a friend would not do what they do'.

Anni Rainbow also contributed insights into the structure of CAAB, which partly answer some of the questions raised earlier in this account about how far it provides a model for similar campaigns. She agreed that it is essentially an informal structure, with no formal membership other than those individuals who contribute financially on a regular basis. (Christine Dean, the volunteer treasurer of CAAB confirmed this and the relatively small annual budget, around £2000, on which it is run.) Support and challenge came essentially from within the small group of campaign workers, local concerned Quakers, and from experienced Quakers from Northern Friends Peace Board. The workers in the campaign were not an isolated group in terms of thinking and approach, and shared experience and information regularly with kindred groups both in Britain and overseas.

When Anni was asked to reflect on what she was most proud of in her years with CAAB she chose the success of the campaign to use the US flag as a means of protest, which she believes was due to Lindis Percy's persistence in the courts. To Anni, this was important because, having rejected the idea the idea of burning the US flag, which seemed a violent action with echoes of Nazis burning books, they settled on writing messages on US flags and/or holding them upside down. This is an internationally accepted form of signalling distress and she felt that it is a powerful tool in communicating their distress at what is happening on US bases. 'We always tried to get information into the public arena, it is not about violence but empowerment.'

Researchers who may, in future use the CAAB records for information on a non violent peace campaign at the turn of the twenty-first century, will find that files of carefully amassed information, researched, evaluated and summarised with integrity, bear witness to the quiet dedication and persistence of Anni Rainbow and Christine Dean, as participant and treasurer to the campaign.

Lindis Percy

Inevitably, the content of this account of CAAB has focussed on the visible challenges both on US bases and in long running-court campaigns in which Lindis Percy has been the front runner. The most significant impression to emerge from any reading of the CAAB records is the particular experience, knowledge and competence in conducting cases in the courts, which this long campaign has enabled Lindis Percy to develop. The evaluation accounts recounted above all comment on the credibility and confidence that made her a formidable adversary in many contexts. Her involvement in CAAB was pursued while still continuing to work part-time as a health visitor in inner Bradford. Despite the number or arrests, court cases and prison sentences she was able to retain her professional career, a fact that she attributes to being throughout, open and honest with management about her activities.

Lindis Percy acknowledged that the focus that CAAB chose is an extremely challenging one in personal terms, and that she would caution young activists about the costs of choosing this route. Her view was consistent with the opinion expressed by Gandhi about the costs of non-violent protest, quoted at the start of this account (see p.11). She advised that challenging and confronting the law may be exciting but on occasion one may also be arrested and end up in custody. Her experience is that, contrary to English perceptions that we value equality before the law, the law is actually relatively inaccessible to the average citizen, that we do not know our rights and can find it hard to explain our position in court in a way that fits in with court procedures. She also stressed that the financial costs are high, especially with the cessation of Legal Aid. This means that the campaigner acts as litigant in person, requiring knowledge of arrest, charge and court procedure which can be very intimidating. In this complex and challenging legal area Lindis looked back at those, particularly John Bugg who taught her about the issue of military bye-law legality, and admits that sometimes 'she got it wrong'. She looked back, too, with gratitude to the local Friends and other campaigners who came to support her during her court appearances and, she believed, themselves learned what happens when courts and the law fail to support the citizen.

A case which for Lindis Percy paid a very high personal price and which also illustrates the importance of knowledge of the law and of the systems in which it is embedded, is what is known as 'the Holloway case'. The following account of this case is drawn solely from an interview with the campaigner.

In 1998 following a temporary injunction to stop Lindis Percy from trespassing at Menwith Hill and infringing the bye-laws, Lindis breached this by marginally stepping off the disputed path there. A warrant was issued later for her arrest while she was abroad, and on her return and following voluntary contact with the local police, she was escorted to Birmingham by bailiffs so that the case could be heard by the original judge who had reserved the case for himself. Before her journey south she was remanded in custody overnight in Hull and, because she was suffering from an acute ear infection was taken from there, in handcuffs, to Hull Royal Infirmary. After the hearing, the judge ordered her to be taken to Holloway prison to await the next hearing. Some elements of Lindis' account of her treatment in Holloway are collaborated by the report by the then H. M. Inspector of Prisons, Sir David Ramsbotham. Sir David published in 1997 a major thematic review entitled Women in Prison, to which Lindis Percy contributed. As a matter of routine she was ordered to be strip-searched on arrival and, when she declined this because of her medical condition resulting from the infection in both ears, was later taken to a closed cell where she was forcibly stripped by five female officers with a nurse standing by. She was then left naked on the floor of the cell. Lindis' account of her reaction to this treatment is plainly close to what is known about responses to traumatic stress. She refused to eat and says that this was not as an act of protest, but simply that she could not allow any further invasion of her body. She was subsequently referred to the prison psychiatrist who could find no evidence of mental disturbance. Meanwhile, her family and CAAB had instructed a lawyer, Mark Stephens (see above), to apply for her release. Professor Roger Higgs, an academic lecturer in General Medical Practice and, among other positions, deputy head of the Division of Primary Care and Public Health from 1998 to 2004, was brought in for a second opinion by her family. Ironically, in order to be seen by the independent medical officer she had to be interviewed by the governor and routinely strip searched again. The subsequent report from Professor Higgs spoke of 'traumatic treatment' and of 'gratuitous violence'. The Official Solicitor applied to have her released and the case was then heard by the original judge who reluctantly agreed to her release. Lindis Percy's supporters and family had arranged for BBC news to be waiting to interview her at the steps of the court, but perhaps because of bureaucratic inefficiency, no paper to release her was available. She was therefore taken back to Holloway and prepared to go through the routine admission procedures, which included being strip-searched again. Dramatically at the last moment she was released due to a high-level intervention by Mark Stephens who contacted the prison governor directly, promising civil action if she was not released immediately. She was instantly released.

The aftermath of these two months in Holloway and the physical conditions and inhumane treatment encountered there clearly affected the campaigner seriously. Lindis Percy needed counselling to address the experience of assault and intimidation, and suffered many of the acknowledged symptoms of Post Traumatic Stress Disorder. There are some positive outcomes to this case, not least her participation in the report 'Women in Prison' already mentioned which recommended banning strip-searching as a matter of routine, her contribution to the 'Women in Prison' campaign, and her correspondence with the Central Council for Nursing and Midwifery about the status and professional responsibility of the nurses who witnessed her strip searches. The case raises the issue of the disproportionate nature of the state's response to what was essentially the civil and not criminal act of trespass, and disturbing awareness of what the outcome might have been might have been had Lindis Percy not had the sustained and effective support of CAAB and of her family, and of many other supporters, known and unknown.

Chapter 8

Looking ahead: What peaceful campaigners can learn from this account

It has been demonstrated throughout this book that the issues continually raised by CAAB are important at any time but the events of 2013 mean that suddenly they are at the centre of debate here, in Europe and in the US. It is therefore important that a campaign that has as its focus the issues of electronic surveillance, democratic oversight, national sovereignty, and the impact on civil liberties should continue to be effective. There are important questions of how the campaign can survive and grow, and how it can be helped to do this.

One way of approaching this is to use an analytical method drawn from the field of conflict analysis and conflict resolution. It provides a tool for analysis that has proven usefulness in working with conflict at domestic, local, national and international levels. It is a systematic approach which aims to understand as fully as possible what is going on in a particular conflict, to identify areas where more knowledge is needed, to assess past efforts and to find ways in which future intervention can be effective. This approach is useful at any stage of a conflict, but especially so in a situation where a lot is known about a conflict but where the party or parties are becoming unfocussed or discouraged. The author's own judgement is that this exercise is particularly relevant to CAAB at this point, can be useful for most non-violent campaigners, and provides a very useful framework within which the achievements and weaknesses of the campaign can be analysed, and a platform for future action considered.

The particular tool chosen for this analysis is that of 'conflict mapping'[72]. This is a technique that maps a conflict graphically. Ideally it would be used in a situation where both parties acknowledge the destructive effects of a conflict and want to work out a negotiated outcome. In this discussion of CAAB's current position, it is used more as a useful way of helping one party to analyse the situation in as objective a way as possible. Conflict mapping requires the analyst, or more usually analysts, to attempt a challenging approach. It requires them to: *describe the conflict from different points of view, including that of their own.* It maps, usually visually, the *parties to a conflict, their relationship with each other, and where the power lies in that relationship.* The analyst is also required to *check the range of its organisation's activities, to see where potential allies might be.* Importantly it encourages the analyst to consider how its organisation and activities are perceived by others, and to enter the values and mindsets, needs and fears, that lie behind the viewpoints which differ from their own. This exercise is not a 'once for all' activity but rather needs to be regularly used as circumstances and knowledge of the situation changes. Importantly it *starts the process of deciding on active intervention, identifying where are the openings for action.*

139

It is obvious that this book has not been describing a conflict in the conventional sense of the term, although it is full of instances of confrontation and often of violence, not always physical. For the purpose of this exercise the following definition of conflict has been adopted: 'a situation between two or more parties (individuals, groups, organisations or states) who have, or think they have, incompatible goals'. Just as in the long-lasting campaigns against slavery, or against the use of child labour in nineteenth century Britain, there are no easily identifiable 'parties' to the conflict. In this campaign the simplest formulation is that the conflict lies between, on the one hand, a campaigning group, not necessarily unique, that has clearly defined aims, methods and objectives, and on the other, economic and political structures and institutions which are in opposition to its aims. It will also be obvious that the analyst here is not one of the parties to the conflict, but an independent researcher who has had no active involvement in the campaign, and who is relying on the records of the campaign, and personal interviews with the campaigners, for the information on which to base the analysis. The mapping exercise requires the analyst to work through some key questions:

1. What is the history and back ground to this conflict?

2. What parties are involved in this conflict or have a serious interest in its outcome?

3. What key bodies or institutions exert power and influence?

4. What significant changes have there been in the political and social background, which need to be taken into account?

1 The history and background

A clear achievement for CAAB has been its uncovering of the secretive and legally unclear nature of the status of US bases in Britain. The painstaking collection of information, the use of parliamentary questions and the key legal cases outlined in this account clarify the issues for legal sovereignty, both in terms of what goes on in the bases, of who has ultimate control and how far its personnel are subject to English law. The campaign has shown how this issue has its roots in the nature of the political relations between Britain and the US from post-World War Two until the post-9/11 era, and how radical changes in US foreign policy and military planning have powerfully impacted on British national interests. These issues are not yet widely seen as significant, although the events of 2013 suggest that the themes of secret surveillance and democratic accountability are emerging as important. The official response to questions about the presence of US bases in Britain usually rests on the argument that their legitimacy lies in the NATO Agreement of 1951 to which the US is party, and which is seen as vital to our defence in the context, first of the Cold War, and now in an era of 'international terrorism'. From that perspective the work of CAAB is seen as at best irrelevant and at worst as a threat to national security. Baroness Williams (see interview above) thought that parliamentarians are very interested in the issue of US bases but are much less concerned with arguments about nuclear disarmament and pacifism.

This gives a useful perspective when we reach the later stage of considering where the future focus for CAAB could be.

2 Who are the main parties involved in this conflict and what other parties have a serious interest in its progress and outcome?

The value of this stage in the mapping exercise is that it requires the analysts to look beyond the individuals or groups with whom they have most interaction, and to see them as part of an often changing network of relationships, obligations and values, which govern their overt actions and policies and which are often hidden. An example of this, but in a local context, would be of youth workers aiming to reduce individual attacks and murders in a neighbourhood and focussing on individuals and families, but without acknowledging the meaning and significance of gang membership, of the shadowy power of drug providers, or of the wider issues of poverty, lack of access to paid work or appropriate education or policing policy. The exercise yields a complex picture but it prevents the campaigner or worker from adopting a naive or narrow focus, or one which is ultimately only partially successful.

The CAAB records enable us to see that the presence and maintenance of US bases in Britain is supported by a cluster of interests and institutions, some of which have been directly targeted by CAAB, and most of which have plainly a very strong interest in the issues raised by the campaign. We can see that the campaigners have had, at the human level, direct contact with MOD and local police, with RAF liaison officers and US security personnel, with the legal profession and the courts at all levels, with parliamentarians and other peace campaigners, with journalists and, to an extent, with the general public. The exercise requires the analysts to locate these individuals in their respective work/professional groups/organisations/institutions and to clarify what are their particular values and interests in relation to the issues raised by the campaign, and what is the nature of the relationships, if any, between each of these groups. Could there be any overlap of interest between each group and CAAB? The process of carrying out this analysis is both complex and illuminating, and the purpose is both to uncover the reality of how each group operates in reality as opposed to its public statements, and to use this information to inform the campaigns' actions and to enable it to decide where to target the work. It also can give useful insights into who might have common interests with the campaign even if this is not immediately obvious.

For example, we can see from the CAAB records that whatever the public website of the Ministry of Defence may say about the functions and legal basis on which its police work, in fact there is evidence of real confusion among its officers when faced with peaceful protestors, about what they can legally do. This is compounded by the responses at the local police station and afterwards at all levels of the legal process. This is not intended to be a blanket condemnation, as the book has already indicated, and we can only guess at the issues involved in working in a setting where one's paymasters are from a different culture. In terms of this exercise the unwillingness of the MOD police to be interviewed for this research means that we cannot begin to answer these questions, or to have a sense of whether the

CAAB campaign and the issues it raises has had an impact on the perceptions and practices of the MOD. There may be some common interests, even at the most basic human level, which could be the first step to a more constructive way of relating to peace protestors. What has been the cost to them of twenty years of confrontation? Could they envisage a different way? Is change possible? Are their energies better focussed elsewhere? Could the sensible accommodation at the Tuesday demonstrations described by the campaigners have been reached earlier and to mutual advantage?

Other significant bodies who would be included in this preliminary analysis would be the media (press, TV, radio, websites and other social networks). The records indicate valuable relationships built up with individual and influential journalists, the importance of which is shown in the interviews. Questions of whether energy should be devoted to developing these relationships rest partly on decisions about the future focus of the campaign. It would also be important to include in the analysis bodies which could be potentially influential such as the Trades Unions and the mainstream churches.

3. What other institutions exert power and influence?

It is possible to identify other institutions that seem to wield a powerful if hidden influence on many of the key events in this campaign. The role of the Crown Prosecution Service has been evident on many occasions. A task for the mapping exercise would be to understand this institution more clearly, its legal functions, its staff, its workload and in particular what, if any, political influences are brought to bear when legal cases that relate to security and intelligence issues are raised by peace campaigners. Throughout the research we have seen instances of the way in which the government of the day and the intelligence and security services have exercised covert influence. Here CAAB is only one body among many who have contributed to a key debate at the turn of the twenty-first Century on the relative ignorance of Parliament on security and intelligence issues. The Scott report of 1996 focussed on the issue and on the hidden power and influence of commercial and intelligence interests in democratic processes. These are fundamental issues for the nature of parliamentary democracy in Britain, and CAAB has been a small voice along other bodies such as 'Liberty' in contributing to this debate.

Plainly, a most powerful country with an interest in the issues raised by CAAB is the US itself. The research has already shown how effective CAAB has been in focussing on the development of US bases in Britain and in particular on the increasing intelligence and strategic importance of Menwith Hill. They have shed a small spotlight on how US security personnel react when confronted with peaceful protestors and on a key issue of national sovereignty, that is whether they are subject to English law. We are beginning to see what is the nature of the perceived gains to Britain in terms of intelligence-sharing and mutual defence, and to be clearer about the potential dangers for Britain, particularly over such serious questions as to whether Menwith Hill would be used to provide the intelligence for drone attacks by the US and how vulnerable this would render the base in times of international tension. We are also seeing the reality of the extent of British control over operational use of these bases, and the increasing controversy about the impact of the 'special relationship' on foreign perceptions of British independence and integrity.

4. What outside factors need to be taken into account?

It is important to locate the campaign in a period of significant social and political change. In the last twenty years there have been developments that have significantly changed the political climate, some of which are of enormous importance. World-wide there are the issues of climate change and the resulting impact on patterns of migration. In Europe, Britain and the US we have seen political and economic crises with an accompanying growth in levels of social inequality[73]. In Britain an accompanying sense of crisis in the competence and incorruptibility of its economic and political institutions are new and important developments. There is a sense that traditional methods of protest are no longer effective, as indicated by the lack of impact on political decision-making of the mass demonstrations at the time of the Iraq war. It is noteworthy that the membership of CND has declined since the end of the Cold War, and that a MORI poll of 2005 indicates that only 1 in 4 of the population shares its views on nuclear weapons. Yet CND's policy of opposing US bases is thought to be in tune with popular opinion. A significant poll conducted by YouGov in 2012, of 12,693 adults across the US, Britain, Europe, the Middle East, North Africa and China on attitudes to the US, reveal that of British participants 40% chose 'bullying' as a word they associated with the US, and 41% of the respondents said they did not trust America. It is not a simple matter to make coherent sense of these major trends in a way that clarifies their significance for CAAB. The purpose of the exercise is to ensure that significant broader trends are included in decisions about future policy.

In summary, the mapping exercise shows a large number of institutions, each with its own values and perceptions, operating within its own legal and constitutional framework. Of these, CAAB is one, and therefore merits the same analysis.

If we look at the organisations and institutions included in the map, are there any that could be identified as sharing some common interests or concerns with CAAB? If so, how might they be engaged? Are there any organisations where it is unrealistic to expect significant change or engagement? Are there any organisations that might be important allies for CAAB (for example CND, Liberty, the Trades Unions) What has CAAB's experiences with these bodies been so far? Are there disadvantages to a closer working or even organisational relationship?

Looking to the future

Following the mapping exercise there are some serious questions that CAAB has to consider and which are pivotal for the future of the campaign. Many of these questions are useful for any similar campaigning body or organisation which is at a critical point in its development and which is ready to reappraise its aims and achievements.

One significant achievement of the campaign has been to contribute, from its own experience and from the ensuing court campaigns, to a public debate on civil liberties and the right to peaceful protest. This experience has clearly been enormously costly in terms of time and personal pain. Should this continue to be a prime focus or could these challenges now be left to larger organisations such as those which reported to the Select Committee of the House of Commons? If this was agreed what would be CAAB's main focus in the next stage of its campaigning?

CAAB has been distinctive in undertaking legal challenges that have specifically focussed on the status and unaccountable activities of US bases in Britain, both regarding their personnel and their changing military and intelligence functions. It has worked with other campaign groups such as CND, with journalists and with other groups world-wide with similar concerns. How does CAAB see the focus of this aspect of the campaign in the future? Is it to work towards a continuing detailed analysis on the network of US bases in Britain? If so, is this best done by groups working in the locality of the bases? Or by looking towards a more academic and research-based approach to the subject? Which method of campaigning does it regard as having been most successful in uncovering the nature of US bases? Are there other organisations and investigative journalists who could be useful allies? One of the journalists interviewed thought CAAB could extend its web-based campaign. What would be the implications for its staffing and organisation?

A major weakness for CAAB may be seen to be the difficulty it has experienced in making a significant impact on public awareness of the functions of US bases in Britain, of their dangers, of their implications for British sovereignty or of the impact on perceptions of Britain in Europe and world-wide of the uses to which they might be put. Nor has official government policy on the importance of the 'special relationship' been modified. However the YouGov research on public attitudes to the US, and the comment by one of the parliamentarians on MP's interest in the issue, suggests that this is a subject where opinions are to some extent fluid. A key question here is whether CAAB now sees itself as set for a long-term political campaign for the abolition of the bases, or whether it could conceive more limited aims, for example, a position where the informal and secretive nature of these bases is opened up to a publically debated, democratically accountable and legally- agreed arrangement. A moment's reflection on the list of bodies with an interest in this issue, including the secretive intelligence community, stops any naive assessment that this would be a short-term or easy campaign, and the likelihood of success and the need for constant review of progress would have to be considered. One of the weaknesses of this book has been the difficulty of gaining a clear assessment of the impact of CAAB's campaign from persons who themselves have reasoned and well-based arguments in favour of the presence of US bases in Britain. It would be of real interest to hear this debate explored and re-evaluated in the light of more current information about the status and workings of US bases. If this were a realistic project, how would CAAB move towards initiating it? Who might be its supporters?

Some fundamental questions have surfaced during this campaign that are not unique to it alone and which underpin its moral foundations. Some of them were raised at the afore-mentioned seminar of 2000 at Bradford University, which demonstrated the importance to any campaign of having contributions and effective criticism from experts who are sympathetic to the campaign but prepared to see its weaknesses. At this seminar important questions were raised as to how campaigners can justify breaking the law. It is clear from the records that the campaigners focussed mainly on testing unsafe law, or law that was unclear in its definition and implementation, and that the court verdicts often vindicated their actions. But on occasions they broke the law for example in disobeying injunctions. How can this be justified, and should there be clear rules and guidelines when campaigners plan to do so? If it is justifiable, can the state claim similar justification, for example to safe-guard public safety?

In deciding on a future focus for the campaigning activities a key question emerges from the body of this research, as to the nature of CAAB as an organisation. Essentially an informal body with a heavy reliance on voluntary workers, small finances and an informal 'management' group that calls on expert advice when needed, the personalities and endurance of its campaigners have been of key importance. Will this continue to be an appropriate? How is the accountability and effectiveness of the campaign to be monitored? Does the current structure need to change if the campaign adopts a different focus? Should it aim for more stable funding? Will new skills and expertise need to be recruited? And, crucial in all organisations on the cusp of change, how can the political, campaigning and legal skills be passed on in a coherent and structured way?

The main function of the mapping exercise is to enable campaigners to move from the mass of information about the groups and institutions that have significance in the campaign to a sharper and more focussed plan of intervention, which incorporates timescales, a strategic plan for the organisation and provision for regular reviews of progress. The Joseph Rowntree Trust devised a series of questions for campaigners applying to the Trust for backing for individual projects[74]. They are in many ways complementary to the questions already raised and can provide a useful starting point for thinking about the future for CAAB or of any comparable campaigning body.

What is your vision for the next five years? What resources will you need? How will you know if you are making progress? What are the risks? What will the challenges be and how will you overcome them? What will you need in terms of skill and expertise which are different from what you have already displayed? Will you need to recruit new 'experts' for this next stage? Is this best pursued as sole workers or as part of an organisation? What sort of organisation will that be? Does it need to change? Do you need to consider how your campaign relates to others with similar aims?

These questions, along with those raised by the mapping exercise, can only be considered by the campaigning organisation itself, perhaps most effectively with the help of outside strategic thinkers brought in for this stage of the campaign's development. The responses of the campaigners to these questions show that some of these issues are already being considered, particularly in relation to the long-term aims of CAAB. This is seen by both Lindis Percy and Martin Schweiger as being the closure of US bases in Britain and the return of US personnel to within their own borders, although they agree that this is likely to take at least a further generation to achieve. The weight of evidence described throughout this book, and the views of respected political commentators, agree that the particular relationship between the US and the UK, the importance of Menwith Hill to US intelligence and defence strategy, and the lack of any real parliamentary oversight and public debate make such an outcome in Britain unlikely in the foreseeable future. This does not rule out a shorter-term goal of renegotiating the terms and status of US bases, following an informed and open debate at public and parliamentary levels, as has happened in other European countries. Once this is clarified it begins to be clear where the focus of campaigning would be and what structure of organisation would be needed.

This book has tried, in its detailed description of the activities of CAAB, both to record and preserve the activities of a significant campaign, to enable other campaigners to learn from its methods and outcomes, and to help to bring it to the point where it can make informed, principled and strategically effective decisions about how it will take forward its experience and learning to achieve its long-term aims. The events of 2013 have stimulated a public debate, to some extent here in the UK but with more vigour in the US and in Europe. With revelations about the democratically unaccountable use of electronic surveillance, what it is used for, what laws exist to prevent abuse, and how elected bodies exercise effective oversight, the insights gained by the activities of CAAB have a real contemporary significance. An effective and carefully considered reappraisal of its future is therefore of real importance at the start of the twenty-first century.

Acknowledgements

I am very grateful to the following, who contributed their time and professional experience to provide thoughtful evaluation of the campaign:

Fabian Hamilton	MP for Leeds NE constituency
Peter Lazenby	Journalist with the Yorkshire Post
Wing Commander Mick Marsh	RAF Commander at Greenham Common, 1983 to 1986
and Ann Marsh	
Baroness Sue Miller	Liberal Democrat peer, House of Lords
Richard Norton-Taylor	Security Editor, 'The Guardian' newspaper
Paul Rogers	Professor of Peace Studies, University of Bradford

Dr. Martin Schweiger	Health Protection Agency, Leeds
Mark Stephens	Stephens Innocent LLP, London W1

The campaigners

Lindis Percy	Joint Coordinator of CAAB, 1992 to present day
Anni Rainbow	Joint Coordinator of CAAB, 1992 to 2006
Christine Dean	Treasurer, CAAB, 1992 to 2012

Financial Support

I am also indebted to the following bodies who contributed financially towards the cost of publication of this book:

Quaker Outreach in Yorkshire

Leeds Area Meeting Finance and Trusts Committee

The Sir James Reckitt Charity, Hull

And to many private individuals who have given time and money in support of this project.

References

Chapter 1 The campaign: background and origins

1   Quaker Faith and Practice: (1994). *The Book of
     Christian Discipline of the Yearly Meeting of the religious
     Society of Friends (Quakers) in Britain.* **(QFP)**

2.   For an introduction to this subject see particularly:

     Galtung, J. (1989) *Solving Conflicts: a Peace Research
     Perspectiv*e. University of Hawaii Press.

     Curle, A. (1971) *Making Peace.* Tavistock, London

     Curle, A. (1999) *To Tame the Hydra.* Jon Carpenter.
     Oxford

Chapter 2 The campaign in context. Non-violence, Civil Liberties, the Quaker connection

3.   Kurlansky, M. (2007) *Non Violence. The history of a
     dangerous idea.* Vintage Press

4.   Curle, A. (1995) *Another Way. Positive responses to
     contemporary violence.* Carpenter. Oxford.

     Lederach, JP. (1995) *Preparing for Peace.* Syracuse, NY.

     Galtung, J. (1996) *Peace by peaceful means.* Sage,
     London.

5. Curle, A. (1995) sup.cit

6. Curle, A. (1989) sup.cit

7. Lederach. JP. (1997) *Building peace. Sustainable Reconciliation in divided societies.* Washington, US.

8. Fetherston, AB and Parkes AC. Transforming violent conflict: contributions from social theory. *Issues in Peace research 1997/8.* University of Bradford p 48.

9. Kurlansky, M (2007). Sup. cit. p152.

10. Wilson, B. (2009) *What Price Liberty?* Faber and Faber, London p 95

11. Ibid, p263.

12. EP Thompson quoted in Wilson (sup cit) p 95.

13. Wilson, B. sup.cit

14. Ibid p46

15. Ibid p97

16. Gearty, C. (2007) *Civil Liberties* Oxford.

17. Wilson, B. sup cit

18. Wilson, B. sup cit p74

19. Judt, T. (2010) *Ill Fares the Land.* Allen and Lane.

20. Ibid 'Conclusions'.

21. Wilson, sup cit p 412

22. Sampson, A. (2004) *Who Runs this Place? The Anatomy of Britain in the 21st Century.* John Murray.

23.   **QFP** sup cit.

24.   Ibid

25.   Ibid

26.   Ibid

27.   Ibid

28.   Ibid 24.04

29.   Ibid 24.21

30.   Ibid 24.24

31.   Ibid 20.46

32.   Ibid 23.36

33.   Ibid 19.59

34.   Ibid 29.12

35.   Ibid 29.11

36.   Whitling, S. *The Friend,* Jan 10 2011

37.   Mendel W. In **QFP**, sup cit 24.22

38.   Gee, D and Hughes, H. (2004) *US Missile Defence: Ten Reasons for UK Concern.* Quaker Peace and Social Witness

39.   Hirst, M. (1923) *The Quakers in Peace and War.* The Swarthmore Press.

40.   *The Friend,* September 2010

41.   Ibid January 21 2011

42.   Mendel, W. **QFP** 24.12

43. Yarrow, M. (1978) *Quaker Experiences in International Situations.* Yale UP

44. Phillips, B. *The Friend,* Jan 21 2011

45. **QFP** 13.02, 13.08, 13.12

46. Bailey, S. (1993) *Peace is a Process.* The Swarthmore Lecture, publ. Quaker Home Service.

Chapter 3 US Bases in Britain: the importance of Menwith Hill

47. Yorkshire CND Report (2012) *Lifting the Lid on Menwith Hill*

48. Campbell, D. 1988. *New Statesman.* ' Somebody's Listening'.

    Campbell, D. 1984. *The Unsinkable Aircraft Carrier. American Military Power in Britain.* Michael Joseph.

49. 'The Guardian' 29/7/98

50. ibid 16/12/2010

51 ibid 12/12/2010

52. Sampson, A. Sup cit pp366-367

53. Hennessey, P. (1996) *Muddling Through. Power, Politics and the Quality of Government in Post-War Britain.* Victor Gollancz, London.

54. Campbell D. and Forbes, P. New Statesman 13/9/1985

ERRATA: REFERENCES

Chapter 7 Towards Evaluation

67   Smith, L. (2009) sup cit ref. 62

68   Smith, L. ibid

69 (in text 71)   Mendel, W. (1974) sup cit ref. 37

Chapter 8 Looking Ahead

70 (in text 72)   Fisher, S et al (2000) *Working with Conflict. Skills and Strategies for Action.* Zed Books UK

71 (in text 73)   Picket, K and Wilkinson, R. (2010) *The Spirit Level. Why Equality is Better for Everyone.* Penguin

72 (in text 74)   Report of the Centenary Project of the Joseph Rowntree Charitable Trust (2005-2010) (2011) York Publications

Chapter 4 The Court campaigns: 1

55. Gearty, C (2007). Sup.cit

Chapter 5 The Court campaigns: 2

56. 'The Guardian' 5/10/94

57. Brooke, H. (2011) *The Secret State: Secrets, surveillance and the Myth of British Democracy.* Windmill Books.

58. ibid p256

59. ibid p259

60. ibid p 253

61. 'The Observer' 4/2/2001

62. Smith, L. (2009) *Voices against War* Mainstream Publishing Co. Edinburgh p216.

Chapter 6 Peaceful Witness

63. Zelter, A. (ed) (2008) *Faslane 365.* Luath Publishing, Edinburgh

64. ibid pxiv

65. ibid, pxiv

66. ibid, chapter 9

Chapter 7 Towards Evaluation

67. Smith, L. sup cit

68. ibid

69. Report of the Centenary Project of the Joseph Rowntree Charitable Trust (2005-2010) (2011). *Visionaries for a Just and Peaceful World*. York Publications.

70. Yorkshire CND Report sup cit

71. Mendel, W. (1974) sup cit p101.

Chapter 8 Looking ahead

72. Fisher, S et al (2000) *Working with Conflict. Skills and Strategies for action*. Zed Books, UK.

73. Picket, K and Wilkinson, R. (2010) *The Spirit Level. Why Equality is Better for Everyone*. Penguin.

74. Report of the Centenary Project. sup. cit. *ref.69*.

Bibliography

Bailey, S. (1993) *Peace is a Process*. The Swarthmore Lecture. Quaker Home Service

Broadhead, L. ed. (1997) *Issues in Peace Research 1997-8*. Dept. of Peace Studies, University of Bradford.

Brooke, H. (2011) *The Secret State. Secrets, Surveillance and the Myth of British Democracy*. Windmill Books.

Campbell, D. (1988) *New Statesman*. 'Somebody's Listening'.

Campbell, D. (1984) *The Unsinkable Aircraft Carrier. American Military Power in Britain*. Michael Joseph.

Curle, A. (1971) *Making Peace*. Tavistock, London.

Curle, A. (1995) *Another Way. Positive responses to Contemporary Violence*. Jon Carpenter, Oxford.

Curle, A. (1999) *To Tame the Hydra*. Jon Carpenter, Oxford.

Fetherston, AB and Parkes, AC. *Transforming Violent Conflict: contributions from Social Theory*. In Broadhead (ed) sup cit.

Fisher S et al. (2000) *Working with Conflict. Skills and Strategies for action*. Zed Books UK.

Galtung, J. (1989) *Solving Conflicts: a Peace Research Perspective*. Univ. Of Hawaii Press.

Galtung, J. (1996) *Peace by Peaceful Means*. Sage, London.

Gearty, C. (2007) *Civil Liberties*. Oxford.

Gee, D. And Hughes, H. (2004) *US Missile Defence: Ten Reasons for UK Concern*. Quaker Peace and Social Witness.

Hennessy, P. (1992) *Never Again. Britain 1945-1951*. Vintage Books.

Hennessy, P. (1995) *The Hidden Wiring*. Victor Gollancz, London.

Hennessy, P. (1996) *Muddling Through*. Victor Gollancz, London.

Hirst, M. (1923) *The Quakers in Peace and War*. The Swarthmore Press.

Hutton, W. (1995) *The State We're In*. Jonathan Cape, London.

Kurlansky, M. (2007) *Non Violence. History of a Dangerous Idea*. Vintage Press.

Judt, T. (2010) *Ill fares the Land*. Allen and Lane.

Lederach, J.P. (1995) *Preparing for Peace*. Syracuse, N.Y.

Lederach, J.P. (1997) *Building Peace*. University Press, Tokyo.

Mendel, W. (1974) *Prophets and Reconcilers. Reflections on the Quaker Peace Testimony*. Swarthmore Press.

Miall, H., Ramsbotham, O. and Woodhouse, T. (1999). *Contemporary Conflict Resolution.* Polity Press, Cambridge.

Picket, K and Wilkinson, R. (2010) *The Spirit Level. Why Equality is Better for Everyone.* Penguin.

Quaker Faith and Practice (**QFP**) *The Book of Christian Discipline of the Yearly Meeting of the Religious Society of Friends (Quakers) in Britain.* Warwick Printing Co.

Ramsbotham, D. (1997) Women in Prison. UK gov. publications

Joseph Rowntree Charitable Trust (2011). *Visionaries for a Just and Peaceful World.* Report of the Centenary project (2005-2010) York Publications

Smith, L. (2009) *Voices against War.* Mainstream Publishing Co. Edinburgh.

Sampson, A. (2004) *Who Runs This Place? The Anatomy of Britain in the 21st Century.* John Murray.

Wilson, B. (2009) *What Price Liberty?* Faber and Faber, London.

Yarrow, C.H. (1978) *Quaker Experiences in International Mediation.* Yale UP. USA

Yorkshire CND. (2012) *Lifting the Lid on Menwith Hill.*

Zelter, A. (ed) 2008) *Faslane 365.* Luath Pub. Edinburgh

Acronyms

ACPO Association of Chief Police Officers

BMD Ballistic Missile Defence

CAAB Campaign for the Accountability of American Bases.

CAT Campaign against the Arms Trade

CJPO Criminal Justice and Public Order Act (1994)

CPS Crown Prosecution Service

DORA Defence of the Realm Act

ECHR European Convention on Human Rights (1950)

GCHQ Government Communications Head Quarters

MOD Ministry of Defence

MDPGA Ministry of Defence Police and Guarding Agency

MEDACT A global charity focussing on the health charity

MEP Member of European Parliament

NGO Non-Governmental Organisation

NSA National Security Agency (US)

QPSW Quaker Peace and Social Witness

SBIRS Space Based Infra Red System

SIGINT Signals Intelligence

SOCPA Serious Organised Crime and Police Act (2005)

SOFA Status of Forces Act (1951)

VFA Visiting Forces Act (1952)

About the author

Dr. Margaret Nunnerley's professional background is in training and teaching in the mediation and conflict resolution fields. Her post-graduate study at the Department of Peace Studies, University of Bradford, included a doctoral thesis in inter-cultural mediation.